A Fair Young Curate

A Fair Young Curate

Munich Crisis Year 1938 – A Diary

by

Frank Wain

Edited by

Christopher Wain

Plaustrum Books

Copyright © Christopher Wain 2007
First published in 2007 by Plaustrum Books
4 Plantation Park, Keele, Staffordshire ST5 5NA

Distributed by Gazelle Book Services Limited
Hightown, White Cross Mills, South Rd, Lancaster,
England LA1 4XS

The right of Christopher Wain to be identified as the editor of the
work, and Frank Wain, the author, has been asserted herein in
accordance with the Copyright, Designs and Patents Act 1988.

British Library Cataloguing in Publication Data
A catalogue record for this book is available from the British Library.

ISBN 978-0-9553361-0-2

Typeset by Amolibros, Milverton, Somerset
This book production has been managed by Amolibros
Printed and bound by T J International Ltd, Padstow, Cornwall, UK

"Ah me! I was a fair young curate, then!"

W S Gilbert, *The Sorcerer*

"Last time I heard that song, I was a fair young curate myself!"

F Wain, 1994

Dedicated to Frank's wife, daughters-in-law and grandchildren,

Alison, Beverley, Helen, Jack, Lorna, Megan, Sandra,

and in memory of

Muriel,

with love from Christopher and Julian

List of Illustrations

Introduction

Frank Wain kept a diary for many years as a young man; one section, dealing with his journey to the West Indies in 1942, was published privately in the late 1980s under the title *If Crab No Walk*. What follows is the only other substantial part preserved at his death in 2002, doubtless kept because, covering as it did the time of his ordination as a priest in autumn 1938, it had particular associations for him. We believe it would please him to see this given a wider audience.

It gives a revealing portrait of its young author, but it does more than this. It also gives an interesting sidelight on everyday life in a society waiting to see whether it would be plunged into war for the second time in successive generations. Those who lived through this time of tension were described by Churchill in October 1938 as "our loyal, brave people, who were ready to do their duty no matter what the cost, who never flinched under the strain of last week. I do not grudge them the natural, spontaneous outburst of joy and relief when they learned that the hard ordeal would no longer be required of them at the moment; but they should know the truth. They should...not suppose that this is the end."

Above all, the diary gives a fascinating picture of life in the Church of England, in particular on its Anglo-Catholic wing, at a time when the controversial issues which caused excited letters to the *Church Times* were the importance of fasting before Communion and whether it was permissible to pray for the dead, rather than women priests and 'gay' bishops. If in these more ecumenical times some of the remarks about the Popish clergy and the 'Prots' read uncomfortably, we must remember that it has been said, "The past is another country; they do things differently there."

It should not be assumed that every view expressed would have been endorsed even by the author himself in his maturer years; the editor remembers him in the 1970s remarking nostalgically: "Of course, there are things I would have gone to the stake for once that don't seem very important now..." Although the reference to the stake is an obvious exaggeration, the events of this diary were closer to the period in which Anglican priests were sent to prison for defying the Public Worship Regulation Act and prosecutions took place for such 'offences' as having lighted candles on the altar and the use of the sign of the cross when blessing the congregation, than they are to our own day.

The editor's commentary is marked off from the diary by indentation, except for brief explanations, which are italicised. Most names that appear in the text are identified in the commentary. However, a number of the clergy who are referred to repeatedly are listed at the end, and reference should also be made to that. Occasional misspellings have been silently corrected, and the setting-out of dates has been for the most part standardised; abbreviations and pieces of non-standard grammar have usually been left, as they give a characteristic flavour to the diary, as too have dates expressed in terms of the church calendar.

The editor would like to thank all those who did their best to answer those eccentric questions that came to them by email or by post – Fr David Sherwood and Ted Keeping of Kenton, The Revd Christopher Sims of the Parish of the Holy Cross, Shrewsbury, Mike Morrogh of Shrewsbury School, The Revd Jonathan Riviere of Sandringham, Peter Allwood of Lichfield

Cathedral School, Patricia Styles of the Scouting Association, Canon Charles Taylor of Lichfield Cathedral, Fr Anthony Grant and Hope Greene of Mirfield, Isabel Syed of The Shrine of Our Lady of Walsingham, and Dr Andy Fear of Manchester University who helped out with a quotation from Horace, as well as helpful staff at the John Rylands University Library of Manchester, the Bodleian Library, Lichfield Cathedral Library, Shropshire Archives, Keele University Media & Communications Centre, and Jane Tatam of Amolibros. And finally The Revd. Catherine Lack of Keele University Chapel, who read the typescript at an early stage and who encouraged me with her interest – even though she cannot have approved the author's attitude to the ordination of women!

CMW

Frank Wain
53 Abbey Foregate
Shrewsbury

Vol. 5.

Thursday, 30th June 1938

The annual Sunday School outing. To Barmouth this
year – through a lot of good scenery (Llangollen etc).
Mass at 7.30. Train at 9.40, with S. Mary's, but not
All Saints, as they had a separate one – too many for
the engines (of which we had 2 for part of the way).
I was in such a hurry to wear my new blazer that I
left my tickets behind: much mirth at my expense! But
the College badge was a great attraction with the kids.
The Vicar & Lumley & Fr Mckenzie & I had a 1st
compartment, but after a while Lumley & I made a
voyage of discovery all down the train. The welcome
was most vociferous all the way.

The Vicar was, of course, FW's own vicar, Loughton
Wilkinson, vicar of the Abbey, Shrewsbury. Ramsay
Mackenzie was vicar of St Mary's, Shrewsbury. Ralph Lumley
was at this time curate of the same church; later in his career
he was vicar at the Abbey, and author of a guidebook to the
church.

Arr. 12.40 – the Hewitt family, who are late for everything they have to do with, arrived 10 minutes later on the All Saints train! Lunch of a sort with the Vicar & Mrs W [*Wilkinson*] at a place reeking of cabbage. We counted 6 little Bethels [*Baptist or Methodist chapels*] and one large parish church (not so bad, might be better). Then, after treating Peter Ford to a donkey ride, at which he'd already spent all his own money, & messing about a bit, I met a small crowd & we walked thro' the town & up about 200 steps, to the top of the hill, where we amused ourselves for wellnigh an hour. To wit, Pat & Stan Thomas, Peter Basnett, Kenny Parker, & Valda and Sven Edwards, who showed us the way. There was a fine view of the hills & the estuary – and what a fool I was not to bring my camera – not for the view but for them. They sent a p.c. of the view to Fr Dachtler, with fond hopes that he wd come and see them soon. [*Harold Dachtler was vicar of a parish in north London, but had presumably originated from Shrewsbury. Pat Thomas did subsequently stay with him – see 18th August.*] If we hadn't done this, Barmouth wd have been an exceedingly dull (tho' pretty) spot.

After tea Lumley & I, & a lot of the boys, went on the Bumpers, or Dodge'ems, or whatever they're called, but we cdn't persuade the beneficed clergy to it by any means. Then nothing to do till the train went – which Alan Davidge & Jimmie Hughes nearly missed.

The journey back practically a repetition of the one there, except that the conversation in the clerical coach became more ecclesiastical. Rather sad to notice Fr M's opinion of Mrs W, but she does indeed let herself in for it!

Fr M professed himself delighted to give me a few lessons about saying Mass in September. And also wanted me to be chaplain to the Bp at the centenary service on the 7th – all very well if I get back from Leeds in time. So here we are, & tomorrow is also a day.

Friday 1st July

Yesterday Harcombe was not with us, but instead was busily getting married – it took place at 12 o/c.

What a dreadful book Hodgson's *Grace of God* is – just can't get down to it!

This is Leonard Hodgson, *The grace of God in faith and philosophy. The Bishop Paddock lectures for 1936,* published by Longmans, Green. It certainly sounds pretty dry! According to *The Mirfield Gazette,* Trinity 1936, p.26, it argues that:

> The controversies about Grace are due to the difficulty of maintaining that Christianity is a religion both of utter dependence upon God and of moral effort. The author suggests that the Church needs the protestant doctrine of justification by faith counterbalanced by catholic *ex opere operato* sacramentalism.

Saturday 2nd July

Choirboys' cricket in the afternoon – v Belle Vue C.C. Lost by a couple of runs after declaring.

The number of references to sport in this diary might surprise those who knew FW in later life, when he professed to have no interest in it at all! However, this particular one does not instil confidence in his knowledge and understanding of cricket – since if you have declared and lose (assuming a one-innings match) the margin must be wickets rather than runs. Perhaps it was just a slip!

> Then the Infants' treat, for which I had to leave by 3.30. The vicar left me in charge – which included shepherding them from the P.H. after tea to the vicarage lawn for games. But we crossed all the roads without accident, & then proceeded to enjoy ourselves without restraint. Must say I do enjoy these things!

The P.H. was the Parish Hall, a Victorian brick building at the end of Tankerville Street. It was evidently used for Sunday School and for some services. In later years it was sold, and is now used by the Christadelphians.

> The goldfish in the pool, which I always thought was a myth, put in a welcome appearance. Back to finish off – little Margaret took Alwyn some mulberry leaves from the tree. Met Young, who came in & said he is going to join the F.C.P., since the CU [*Church Union*] is "resting on its laurels".

The Church Union was a High-Church body founded in 1934 by the amalgamation of the English Church Union and the Anglo-Catholic Congress. Its founding chairman had been Lord Halifax, the father of the Foreign Secretary and well-known in ecclesiastical affairs for many years. The F.C.P. was the Federation of Catholic Priests.

He is proposed by Fr Hambling & seconded by Fr Mckenzie. Then I went out to buy some cheesy biscuits to supplement my supper, & heard from Mrs Dickson how the mulberry leaves had produced new life & activity in the silkworms!...

Sunday 3rd July – Trinity III

All very much as usual – preached at the P.H. Rehearsed Peter Ford, who is going to start serving on Tuesdays. Then for a walk by the Brook again. Two new boys at SS [*Sunday School*] – brought along by Peter Barnett. Told the class about S. Winifrid – whole story, including the translation to Shrewsbury, & the remains of the shrine. Then Alwyn, Donald & Bebley came to the vestry to be shown the incense.

St Winifed was a seventh-century abbess from Flintshire who, according to legend, was killed by a frustrated lover, and miraculously restored to life. The eponymous Holy well marks the traditional spot. In 1138 her relics were translated to Shrewsbury, and this provided the background to the first of Ellis Peters' Brother Cadfael novels, *A Morbid Taste for Bones*. St Winifred's cult was very popular throughout the middle ages, and a part of the shrine, broken up at the Reformation, had only recently (1933) been restored to the church from a garden in the town.

The vicarage cat was run over last week, & they now have a new one. Also the maid is leaving, as they have had a crisis about her stealing habits.

Monday 4th July

After lunch called at the Youngs in Whitehall St. for the first time – and then to the Ruridecanal chapter. Dull in parts of course, but Fr Mackenzie & Fr Goodacre were good in their reports about The Assembly & Convocation respectively.

Before the arrival of Synodical Government in the 1960s, the Church Assembly, set up under an Act of 1919, had the responsibility for preparing ecclesiastical measures for transmission to Parliament, but was debarred from pronouncing on theology. Convocation was a similar body, whose origins went back to the Middle Ages, but with no House of Laity.

Then it transpired that it is true about Headlescote still requiring £800 for their church – but the fact is that it cost over £2,000, not £1,000. The vicar of S. Alkmund's appealed for help. [*Glynne Thomas, at this time, though he had left by the end of the period of this diary.*]

On returning I found that I'd missed a visit from Cecil Sayer! Mrs Lloyd [*the landlady*] said "Isn't he nice!!" It is <u>he</u> who is going to Guiana, & he'd been up to see the Bishop at Mrs Mackay's, but had to go by the 5 o/c train. So now he, as well as she, wants <u>me</u> to go there. I <u>almost</u> think p'raps I might, but I do want to stay here for a number of years. Anyway, it is tropical…& the stomach has to be thought of. Cecil is being married before going out – all very well for him, as that girl is a nurse…

The reference to the stomach refers to FW's duodenal ulcer with which he was very seriously ill as a student. It was sometimes said that he was never ill again from that time until he had flu in 1969 – though that was plainly an exaggeration – see 8th July. Cecil Sayer had been at the College of the Resurrection a year before FW, and was now Curate of Malvern Link. In 1939 he became Rector of Anna Regina in the Diocese of Guiana, and in 1946 Principal of Codrington College, Barbados. This entry is interesting in that it foreshadows FW's own work in the West Indies, starting in 1942, in his case in St Vincent in the Windward Islands.

Tuesday 5th July

Last night, dinner at Mrs Mackay's to meet the Bp of Guiana. [*The Rt. Rev. Alan Knight, consecrated bishop 1937.*] Misses Gibb & Young also there, but not Mr Dovey, as <u>he</u> now has a bad throat. A very interesting evening – the Bp's experiences – fully Catholic. He knows Fr Bill Wright – hurray! & had some new stories of him. He was in his purple cassock, & Young greeted him properly, by kissing his ring – to the astonishment of the ladies. I didn't – being too shy! Cecil, he says, wrote to him out of the blue – he doesn't know yet what put the idea of Guiana into his head. "Keep the Catholic flag wagging" said Cecil in a PS to the note he left for me. Very cheering to have that from Cecil. Mrs Lloyd gave him tea & cake.

Today Peter Ford should have served at the early mass for the first time – but was sick yesterday evening, so couldn't. But the child sent his mother round to apologise – the first time a server has been so thoughtful at <u>this</u> church! At the Anson class we got on to the Commonwealth & then Charles II – quite good going.

Under the 1936 Education Act, the law allowed a child to be withdrawn from school during a period of religious instruction if the parents had arranged for him to attend religious observance or instruction elsewhere. The Anson class was named after the Parliamentary Secretary to the Board of Education at the time of the passing of the 1902 Education Act. Evidently FW refers to a time when he had "gone in" to teach in a local school.

That afternoon he went to Mirfield, where he had been trained for the priesthood. In the days before widely-available grants, the Community of the Resurrection had firstly seen him through Leeds University and then given him two years of training at the College of the Resurrection at Mirfield.

After an early lunch, by the 12.50 to Leeds. The usual foul journey, only enlivened by meeting a strange old student at Stalybridge. The new station at Leeds is going to be magnificent – built into the new Hotel. Very fine booking hall – palatial τοποι [*euphemism for "Gents"*]. Tea at Betty's for old acquaintance' sake. Their excellent toasted teacakes & excellent chocolate cakes, & unsurpassed china tea! It rained a lot on the roofs outside, as they'd had quite a lot lately, including a small cloudburst on Friday – did 'em good, no doubt. Later I got mistaken for a popish priest by a beggar. I always go & say a prayer in the Roman cathedral (today they were being redecorated, & were in almost as much confusion as we were at Mirfield 18 months ago), & I couldn't help noticing an M.D. youth, very devout. [*In those politically incorrect times, this abbreviation meant mentally deficient.*] Outside he button-holed me…well, "it is better to lose money than pity". [*A quotation from St Bernard, at least according to FW's commonplace book compiled during the 1930s, though it has also been described as "one of the sayings of St Vincent de Paul". Perhaps they both used it.*] He discussed the weather, father, & was I going to the seminary, father? No, I was staying with friends… . I didn't know Leeds very well. He had to walk home to Horseford, it's a lovely church, S. Margaret's. They didn't ever have tea at his house, well they were all unemployed. And if they were all like him at home, they always would be, but they'd get through the world all right, somehow, & maybe to heaven as well.

In the Hostel was Ronny Moore, [*two years ahead of FW at the College; at this time Acting Curate of Nantwich*] but others soon came; the refec half full at dinner. Fr Frankie appeared in a car to fetch the ornaments from the Hostel Altar – those for the big High Altar are made, but yesterday the chapter unanimously decided that they could not possibly tolerate such atrocities in the church for a moment! Unfortunately the *Church Times* already has a photo of them. We are going over tomorrow in cassocks, owing to the excavated condition of the attiring chamber! About 100 old students in all, all generations & nearly every year being represented. There is one who is the dead spit of Fr Elwin [*Millard – see below under 7th July*]. Ron Jasper has a 2nd, Gordon Dunstan a very good 1st – & the latter is being allowed to accept a research scholarship. [*R C D Jasper was ordained priest in 1941. In later life he was an eminent liturgiolist, chiefly responsible for the* Alternative Service

Book *of 1980, also author of* The development of Anglican liturgy, 1662-1980, *London, SPCK, 1989, and Dean of York from 1975 to 1984. Dunstan was ordained priest in 1942. His subsequent career included spells as Subwarden of St Deniol's Library at Hawarden and a lecturer at the William Temple College.*] Priestner & Crowder are down, alas. Tommy Thompson is through. Sandy is here, girt about the middle with a large chain, but otherwise very much like Jack Hulbert. I am retiring fairly early (10), with a good bath. There is no time limit tonight! [*Added:*] Didn't retire – talked both nights till after Midnight.

Wednesday 6th July

This was the day of the dedication of the Church of the Resurrection, which had been completed as a memorial to Bishop Gore, the founder of the Community. Michael Tapper had succeeded his late father, Sir Walter, as architect. William Temple, the then Archbishop of York, presided at the service. FW's copy of the Order of Service survives amongst his papers.

Up by 6.30 – Mattins and Mass. Breakfast. Then a special bus to Mirfield – 9.30. We arrived with 20 minutes to spare before the dedication of the Church. Impossible to describe the building, but everything just right. The architect (Tapper) was picked up at The Queen's Hotel, & came for the day. As soon as we were seated in the Nave, Dickie Richardson said, "Oh dear, I never come here without feeling I want to come back home." It was an aw[e]ful moment – everything was so overpowering – I had just said "That's the ideal position for Our Lady" – on the step at the side of the Resurrection chapel. Somebody had done <u>all</u> the flowers most beautifully – a novice who is a worthy successor to Fr Barnes. *(Richard Barnes was a middle-aged member of the Community who had evidently passed on the job.)* The Hammond organ was played by Dudley Hill – if one hadn't known, one wd probably <u>not</u> have said it was "wirelessy"! He played, among other things, *Jesu, joy of man's desiring* before, & *The Trumpet Song* afterwards. But it can never have the beautiful tone of the old organ. [*This was evidently a primitive electronic organ – the first Hammond had been made as recently as 1935. Dudley Hill was a contemporary of FW at college, at this time curate of St Mary's, Wellingborough.*] The Archbishop was assisted by 3 assistant bishops – I forget who, and there were others in the choir. Bp Frere's tomb was not ready.

Walter Frere was one of the founding members of the Community of the Resurrection in 1892; he was Superior from 1902 to 1913 and again from 1916 to 1922. From 1923 to 1935 he was Bishop of Truro. He had retired to Mirfield, where he died in April 1938. He was a leading authority on liturgy, and an active promoter of reunion between the Church of England and the Roman Catholic and Orthodox churches. He was also an eminent musicologist, and had completed the drafting of the consecration service a few days before his death. An article signed Dr A E (not a CR member) entitled *Dr Frere's contribution to music* in *The Mirfield Gazette* for Lent 1939, pp.3-7, describes him as a "man whose earthly labours – besides those of his high calling as a devoted servant of God – were given up to the study of liturgical music, and especially to that of Plain-song, a study cultivated but little, and by few who may be ranked with him."

The screen at the back of the choir is obviously needed, to prevent the eye from wandering right to the end of the Resurrection Chapel. Today this was packed with women visitors. The transepts were filled with monks & nuns from other communities. It was a treat to see them all – Benedictines, including the Abbot of Nashdom & Dom Gregory [*Dix – the eminent liturgiologist*]; several from Kelham, several from the S.D.C.; several from Cowley; Brother Douglas & a few Franciscans; several from Alton, including Fr Aidan, with whom I talked at tea; and nuns of all varieties. There were several new faces in the C.R. stall (I mean besides those obviously on furlough from Africa) including 2 or 3 lay novices.

One of the important fields of work of the CR has always been South Africa; its best-known member has been Trevor Huddleston, famous for his work there and for his opposition to the *apartheid* regime. His connection with the Community did not begin until 1939, but FW did later meet him.

The author of an account (signed H d'A C) of the dedication in *The Mirfield Gazette*, Martinmas 1938, pp. 28-29, was also full of enthusiasm:

> One of the most impressive services we have ever seen or have hoped to see. ... May all who helped to create this memorial say, in the words of the Offertory: 'O Lord God of Israel, keep for ever this imagination of the heart of Thy people.'

Lunch was not as good as last year at the College Festival – new caterers, who will not appear again! Coffee afterwards on the House Lawn. My gosh, what a welcome one gets! Fr Blair [*Andrew Blair, later Prior of the Community*] spoke about Bob Acres. Ron Jasper wanted to monopolise me. And so on & so on. After tea (in the House) the Hostel did a special dress rehearsal of the Commem Play for us. How young they all seem. The play was Shaw's *S. Joan* – cut down – asking for disaster – but! It was going magnificently – Delve *(a student, ordained deacon in 1940, priest in 1941)* was S. Joan, & tremendously good. The music between scenes, tho' good (of course) was not a great success.

A review in *The Mirfield Gazette,* Martinmas 1938, pp. 30-31, comments:

It was no new suggestion, this – that the Hostel should perform Shaw's *S Joan* in the Quarry [*an out-door theatre in the grounds of the Community*]. And not the first time that heads were shaken and doubts expressed. Anyway, the outcome was that the play was performed and the result was a very creditable one for Producer, actors and all concerned... . John Delve played the part of the Maid. ... [His] final presentation was entirely satisfying and as an acting achievement was first class. It goes without saying that it was difficult, but apart from subdued laughter at (we believe) Joan's not very modern perm, even the juvenile groundlings were impressed and held. And they are indeed critical of males playing female parts. [*FW had a story of the reaction of a juvenile groundling to his own performance as Wart in* Henry IV Part 2 *in a previous production in 1935!*]

Then I wandered through the Calvary garden & cemetery, & pottered round the Church till it was time for the bus. Pierre Dawson is saying Mass at 7.0 (votive, of Our Lady, as it is a free day), Then for a cup of tea & a sausage roll, & a share in a taxi down to the City Square for the 7.50, hoping it will be in time for the Centenary of the Charter do, at S. Mary's, Shrewsbury. I write this in Gordon Dunstan's room at 9.45. Tomorrow is also a day.

William Athelstan Pierrepoint Dawson was a former student of the College who had been ordained priest two years before, and was a curate at Sydenham.

Thursday 7th July

Noticed yesterday that there was no oil for the consecration ceremonies – it is now suggested that the Abp is shy of it – because the last time he did such a thing it "caused Mr Kensit to spit blood & bring forth fireirons". For the same reason the deacons of honour did the holy water & censing of the consecration crosses.

The original John Kensit, a campaigner against what he believed to be romanizing tendencies in the C of E, (described by the *Dictionary of National Biography* as "a sincere but narrow-minded fanatic") died in 1902, but there were other members of the family still active in the twentieth century.

Story of when a cat appeared from behind the Baldacchino [*the canopy which covers the altar*] & sat calmly washing itself, during Compline, until Fr Ellis pounced upon it.

Story of when Fr Hannay went straight from the 1st Lesson to the Benedictus, & afterwards said "I wondered why Mattins was over so quickly this morning!" Also when he (Tom) sang the *Exultet* at the top of the stepladder on Easter Eve, & dropped one of the grains of incense: "...This holy I-I-incense – oh drat!". The same at *Tenebrae*: "Oh dammitall, hasn't anybody got a match?"

The *Exultet* is sung at the blessing of the paschal candle on Easter Eve. *Tenebrae* is a Holy Week service in which a series of candles are successively extinguished, symbolising Jesus' death and descent into Hades.

When the Superior sang the Preface twice over from beginning to end. (He was very Keblish yesterday).

Edward Keble Talbot was Superior of the CR from 1922 to 1940. He died in 1949.

When Fr Millard (this from himself) came up from London a day early specially to preach to the College, swotted over a sermon in the train, prayed for hours in the Holy Cross chapel, & then walked into the Ascension chapel at the appropriate moment, only to find another preacher just getting into his stride!

Paul Elwin Millard had been a member of the CR since 1914.

When a priest (not C.R.) mixed up the Prayer for the Church "...this congregation here present...truly serving thee, in holiness & righteousness all the days of their life. And thou child shalt be called the prophet of the Highest!!!"

The phrase in the prayer of intercession at Holy Communion may be easily confused by the inattentive with another; "In holiness and righteousness before him: all the days of OUR life" is the phrase which, in the Benedictus, one of the canticles at Morning Prayer, leads on to "And thou, child, shalt be called..."

All this & much more last night at the bottom of the old Wing stairs in the accustomed place.

Rose this morning in good time to receive Communion at Dawson's Mass at 7 o/c. NB how he fluttered & fumbled with the pages of the Missal – to which he is quite accustomed. And how very reverent Freddie Anson was at his, at the High Altar. Elwin & Miss B. were at ours. Then a quick cup of tea & a sausage roll in the refec, & a long wait with one Fr Williams for the taxi he'd ordered for 7.30, which never came! Elwin phoned for another, but it missed the train by one minute. I cd have sworn. Had to telegram Fr Mackenzie. And missed the do at which I was to be Bp's chaplain. I arrived just as it was over, while the bells were ringing magnificently, and saw Lumley. But Fr M was in too big a hurry – changed into shineys for the luncheon at Morris's. Positive he will not forgive such inefficiency! At 53 Bertie Jones was waiting for me, & my lunch was dried up thro' being kept. We had a walk in the Quarry, then tea at Morris's, where the speeches & songs were still continuing, & we met Harold Francis. Saw Bertie off on one bus, & returned with Stephen Othen on another.

The Quarry is a park in Shrewsbury, part of which was originally the source of stone for the first mediaeval buildings, though it is also possible that the name derives from the Welsh word for *play*.

Bertie Jones was a lifelong correspondent of FW, who left a file of his letters and contributions to parish magazines and other publications going through to his death in 1977. They later shared overlapping periods of service in St Vincent, where Bertie's parish was St James, Layou, and FW's St Matthew's, Biabou; it was Bertie who mentioned FW's name "non-committally" to Bishop Tonks of the Windward Islands, as "one with no ties who would be sure to think of it as a call"! (Quotation from *If crab no walk*, p.3.)

The Mirfield Gazette has arrived, & contains two beautiful appreciations of Bp Frere. The second obviously by John Graham. [*An exact contemporary of FW at the College, at this time curate at St John the Evangelist, Middlesborough, he was eventually Superior of the Community, 1958-1965.*]

This *Gazette* was still amongst FW's books at his death. A brief extract from the second appreciation, entitled + *W.F. The last years*:

From the slightest contact one knew he was not merely a learned scholar or a very cultured gentleman nor even just a shrewd and humorous judge of character. He was something inclusive of all and more than all: he was a saint. [*In his preaching:*] There was a breath-taking simplicity, so that one listened charmed, fascinated, spell-bound, helpless with joy. [*His was*]…an intensely attractive, somewhat numinous character, each tiny particle of which was utterly dedicated to the service of God.

FW continued:

> I really am luckier than the great majority of my year – this came out. In spite of snags. Talking of snags, I said to Pierre Dawson (who said "how marvellous", about the Abbey), "the snags appear later, & not the obvious ones either" – & he said "Yes, after about six months", & then, suddenly, "when you find your Vicar isn't a gentleman, when you thought he was". Of course, what Pierre's idea of a gentleman is…

> LATISH, THURS. NIGHT, having got up, being too fed up (partly with myself) to sleep. God help the Church of England. We can't. But he moves in a marvellous mysterious way.

> And now I've smoked too many cigarettes.

This despairing comment about the Church of England calls to mind the remark of Thomas Arnold in June 1832, "The Church as it now stands no human power can save". It is tempting to speculate that FW was at the time conscious of the parallel, as later it was a favourite quotation of his. The point of the story is, of course, that just over a year later began the Tractarian Movement – God's way of saving the C of E, at least according to one interpretation!

Friday, 8th July

> No wonder I was fed up last night – about half an hour after writing the above I was sick – very acid – all the

recent travelling & excitement & changes of food – & neglect of Mclean's powder. Now two days of anxious swotting – for the first time in my life I'm going into an exam unprepared! And there is this blessed missionary pageant rehearsal the night before it!

I ought to have mentioned the other day that Bradford is engaged, & that Scupholme of all people is actually married! How unkind to say "some women wd marry anybody!!" [*Richard Bradford was a year before FW at the College, and by now was a curate in the East End. Albert Scupholme was a year earlier than that.*]

Also that there were a number of communions at the Dedication Mass (CR Brethren). I thought at the time that it was because of the idea of the proper completion of the liturgy, etc – but somebody said it was in order to "gain indulgences" – Fr Viccy discovered the possibility, & Bags [*nickname of Fr Symonds, a great favourite of FW amongst the Mirfield fathers. See later, under 3rd September.*] backed him up...but how much truth there is in the story it would be impossible to say.

Sunday 10th July

The Bp of Guiana said the 8 o/c Mass. Since coming back from Mirfield I've been at sixes and sevens. Maybe "go back home" for good some day! After Mass Mr Adams (who served) asked if he could serve my first mass. So I told him I must have a priest & Young was going to do it. I also asked him to take some of the boys to the ordination in his car, & he was very pleased, but said he must ask his wife first. It's her car! Mem:

to include John Cox – he so rarely gets an outing. Sang Mattins & preached at Cound [*a village a few miles from Shrewsbury*] at 11 – a charming courtly church – evidently more Catholic at one time – 3 altars & an ancient piscina restored. Choir & good congregation (since the Squire sets the local farmers a good example!). The squire also puts £1 note in the collection – thus making it £1:1:1. I gave them The Body of Xt sermon, which always goes down well. Afterwards the organist brought me back – a Lancashire man, who's a master at Harlescote school & night school. After SS [*Sunday School*], Alwyn & a few others came to the Vicarage to get mulberry leaves, since the silkworms, who have grown to a tremendous size, refuse to return to their diet of lettuce! After supper the Vicar told me that the corporation are insisting on having lavatory accommodation at the new church. [*For which see below under 10th August*]. So far so good – but they want separate accommodation – for both sexes! Picture of turning them into Confessional boxes, with a label: FR. YOUNG – VACANT & FR.WILKINSON – ENGAGED!!!

Tuesday 12th July

Last night we had a <u>sort of</u> rehearsal of our part in the Missionary exhibition, but Fr Hambling was ill & unable to come. So Young & Mr Green took charge. S. Mary's were arranged for the same time, and it was refreshing to notice that our people, especially men, turned up much better than theirs!

Alas, my stomach played hell all day – & is still doing

so – I was afraid I might be ill, but it's passing off. LAUS DEO. [*Praise be to God!*] The worst symptoms – blood – after being sick last Thursday night. But I've taken vast quantities of Maclean's & eaten very little. When I get back I'll get some "liquorice powder" & some olive oil, & hope I won't have to go to the doctor. Today, feeling awful, I've come to Lichfield for Part 2 of "priests". Holt at the same fare came via Stafford, which turns out to be quicker. At Wolverhampton I met Creears, who is very happy indeed at S. Peter's. In spite of lack of the outward things, & a certain number of non-fasting communions, they have hosts of genuine Catholics – confession, etc. So should we have, if only the Vicar was "good with" the young people. [*Francis Creears was curate at Wolverhampton, and was ordained together with FW, as will be seen later.*]

At Lichfield I am having a bed at Canon Hammond's, who is much nicer an acquaintance than I ever thought him. Owing to the congenital inefficiency of the domestic chaplain, my arrival this morning was the first he'd heard of it! Breakfast tomorrow, too. [*Canon Lempriere Hammond was a former Vicar and rural Dean of Walsall, and had been a canon of Lichfield since 1934. In 1939 he became Bishop of Stafford. There will be more of the domestic chaplain – see under 29th September and 2nd October.*]

Other meals at the Palace, where we have met two of the innumerable episcopal daughters & are not impressed. [*The bishop and Mrs Woods had three sons and three daughters.*] Also a German visitor. The Bp away in London, & Mrs Bp entertaining in his stead

– & she <u>IS</u> entertaining, unconsciously. The first paper
(NT) was not at all bad. The second, after tea, worse
– on Bevyn's Xnity, [*sic*] but I told 'em a lot, tho' not
out of the book. One cd let oneself expand.

Edwyn Robert Bevan's *Christianity* had been published in
1932, and was a textbook in the Home University of Modern
Knowledge series.

During the first we had our so-called vivas – no ref
whatever to the N.T., but instead a rapid review of the
papers in Part One, most of which he was pleased with.
But the missionary one, being such a "tabulated" book,
I had tabulated it in my mind, & reproduced it in such
a remarkable way that he half suspected I'd had the
book there! It was most unfortunate, but he quite
accepted my explanation, & I think realised how very
genuine my astonishment was! He was very nice,
though he hails from Wycliffe Hall.

A revealing remark! Wycliffe Hall is the leading theological
college on the evangelical wing of the C of E, based at Oxford,
where it received the status of a Permanent Private Hall of
the University in 1996. It had been founded in 1877.

After dinner, for a walk with Creears, beyond Stowe
Pool, S. Chad's well, & to the railway & back, a short
chat with Canon Hammond & his guest, & to bed at
10.30.

That seemed a long walk to FW's elder son, when he did
occasionally walk that far as a schoolboy living in the Cathedral
Close! Perhaps not so long a walk for an adult to take on a

summer's evening as for a reluctant schoolboy on a cold afternoon!

No mass tomorrow, since that at the Cathedral is at 8 o/c & they don't dream of supplying one at the Palace! In the Palace chapel, alas, they have introduced *Songs of Praise*. [*Then known as the name of a hymnbook, rather than a television programme.*]

Wednesday 13th July

A most comfortable night – & much improved. Woke refreshed, for a change. Topping bed – only a small room, but with a view of the west front. And so I was wakened at 6 by the ringing of the bell for Prime. Of course nobody goes, but the wretched verger has to ring for all the Hours! There was even a box of biscuits near the bed, and, in the morning, a cup of tea at the door. I used to associate Lichfield with Dr Johnson, but I'm gradually coming to associate it instead with lukewarm morning baths in beautifully got-up bathrooms. Canon Hammond's is particularly nice. At breakfast I met Mrs Hammond & their son & daughter.

The exam took place at the Bishop's Palace, in the Great Hall – where twenty-five years later FW's elder son was to do exams himself (and both his sons used it for PE on wet days, school assemblies, and the like). The then bishop, Stretton Reeve, decided that the Palace was quite unsuitable for a bishop's residence in post-war conditions, and gave it to be used, from 1954, by the Cathedral School. Many stories follow from that – but they do not belong in this volume!

…We did two two-hour papers in the morning instead of saving one for the afternoon. The Pastoralia was absurd – they were obviously out to see what we thought, to "place" us. And the paper on Hodgson's horrid book was lousy. I answered the questions, & I think satisfactorily, but only rarely did I recollect Hodgson saying anything on the subject! Mrs Woods appeared again at lunch – her old self. No more need be said.

Mrs Woods was the bishop's wife. It is not known whether she deserved the reputation of a Mrs Proudie – tradition around the Close at Lichfield does not support it – but FW seems to have thought so! For what it is worth, *The Times* obituary of one of her children, Janet Stone (Saturday 7th February, 1998), describes her as "eccentric", giving as evidence that she accidentally left her new-born baby in a basket on a train, somewhere between Cromer and Davos. Other tales relate to her stripping the newly-made bed in the guest-room, forgetting that Queen Elizabeth (the future Queen-Mother) was about to come to stay. Altogether, we get an impression of absent-mindedness rather than of bossiness!

Getting away thus early, I stopped in Wolverhampton. The Hassalls were out, so I squinted at the church & noted that they have a Lady Statue. Then a look at S. George's, where I lit a couple of votive candles, & had a free two pennorth of magazine (my invariable custom "in all the churches"). [*The phrase echoes one used in various places in the New Testament.*] They have devotions on Saturday nights, & a new curate. From the notice board, S. James', Wednesbury, appear to be having a magnificent festival, but I shan't be able to go on the 24th, having promised to preach at S. George's Walsall. [*A church he knew from boyhood days. (See below under 24th July.)*]

Then tea, I forget the name of the place, & a look at S. Peter's – in great confusion, scaffolding, etc. If ever there was an altar which needed 6 candles, it's their nave altar. Then the Hassalls were in, & we had a jolly evening, ending with the C.B.S. [*Confraternity of the Blessed Sacrament.*] office in church – much incense. Back in Shrewsbury by the 8.44. While at S. Stephen's, in came Fr Ellis of S. George's, with another priest. They were going round getting the clergy to protest about the Rector of Wolverhampton having Lord Leverhulme, divorced & re-married, to open a big bazaar. Awkward for the Rector as he's an old school pal of his – but he shd have thought of that when he asked him. The Church Union & the Mothers' Union up in arms!

This is the second viscount, the son of the original manufacturer of Sunlight Soap. He was born in 1888, married first in 1912, divorced in 1936 and remarried in 1937 to Winifrid Morris, *née* Lloyd. He died in 1949.

Great relief at the prospect of no more <u>exams</u>, ever! After the holidays I hope to start work for my MA thesis. Forgot to mention that on arriving at Lichfield we had an unexpected treat – I took Creears in to see the chapel at S. John's Hospital, & in the garden we met Fr Wynn Griffith himself – quite active, tho' not as formerly – he must be nearly 90. And he had some witty remarks about when he was taking the exam for Priests!

Ronald Wynn Griffith had been master of St John's Hospital, Lichfield, since 1926, and had been ordained priest as far back as 1882! From 1889 to 1926 he was incumbent of St Andrew's, Birchills, Walsall, where FW was to serve his second curacy, where according to the oral history of the parish, "he was responsible for building up our Anglo-Catholic tradition". He died in 1940. St John's Hospital was a mediaeval foundation, which still has accommodation for elderly people with Anglo-Catholic services in the chapel.

Thursday 14th July

> Stayed in bed this morning, to make a complete recovery, & alas, the Vicar had no one at Mass – even the server, John Cox, usually so reliable, didn't turn up. I didn't ask the vicar whether he said the Mass, in case he said Yes – he's capable of it, & has done so before!

The rubric in the BCP (Book of Common Prayer) says "There shall be no celebration of the Lord's Supper, except there be a convenient number to communicate with the Priest, according to his discretion." The next rubric goes on to define as a minimum number "four (or three at the least)".

> Today Prestfelde School sports – showery, but not thereby spoiled.

Prestfelde is a school in Shrewsbury of the Woodard Foundation – a group of independent schools founded in the nineteenth century with an high Anglican ethos. (See also below on 1st October.)

The Bp of Guiana presented the prizes & said a few words – a couple of marquees on the front lawn – and a good tea, gratis. The boys were fine – wanted to know if I was going there again. Tudor has not shown even Wareham his autograph book! The funniest event was the School Handicap – we never had one at Q.M. [*Queen Mary's Grammar School, Walsall – FW's old school.*] It was like the Caucus Race in Alice – and very difficult to see when they'd finished – the judges had to run round as well, and the big boys let the little ones win.

As described in Chapter III of *Alice in Wonderland*: "There was no 'One, two, three, and away!' but they began running when they liked, and left off when they liked, so that it was not easy to know when the race was over."

Davies G did some excellent jumping (the high jump) but Morrell just managed to beat him. I've written a snorting criticism of Wesley's "Few Hexameters" for *The Mirfield Gazette* – and will probably send it in for Xmas. [*It does not seem to have been published.*]

Friday 15th July

Flicks this evening. Ronald Colman in *The prisoner of Zenda* at the Granada, very good. [*Made in 1937, this also starred Douglas Fairbanks, Junior, as Rupert and Madeleine Carrol as Flavia. A young David Niven also had a part.*] On the way back, a quiet sort of evening by the river. There I met Rawlins of S. Chad's, who asked me to help him by preaching there on Sunday. They have a monthly sung Mass, which he is singing after a very busy morning. So I'm going, in spite of objecting to their 40 or 50 non-fasting communions.

St Chad's was the civic church of Shrewsbury, and not to the taste of a radically Anglo-Catholic curate.

The sort of Bishop we have: July 14th, from *The Times* – presiding at a "welcome to England" for some American preachers, who are going to "exchange pulpits" in "churches & mission halls". A representative of the B. & F.B.S. [*British and Foreign Bible Society – an interdenominational society*] "joined in the welcome". The Bp said they (English & Americans) "had the moral leadership of the world in their hands", omitting to mention that Lord Leverhulme who shd have presided, had been divorced & remarried. "The United States ministers include 4 Episcopalians, 3 Congregationalists, one Baptist, 2 Methodists and 4 Presbyterians" (*The Times*).

TRINITY IV, 1938

After a fairly normal beginning – to S. Chad's, to preach at 11. I was a bit shy about passing the Popish Conventicle in my cassock – & as I drew near they all said Good morning, but as I passed by & my real character became obvious they refrained! At S. Chad's the bells were ringing very fine – not as good as S Mary's, however. And eventually we all processed in – choirboys in red cassocks, men in blue. The church more attractive when in use – four candles & 2 standards at the altar. The choir very squashed, but well disciplined! It's a v. good building for preaching – I enjoyed that part of it – it must be very fine when even the galleries are crowded. [*It is a very striking classical building, opened in 1792.*] But at the communion, I helped with the chalice, and there were nearly 50 communicants – including a few young fellows. It was awful – I told Rawlins I didn't want to come again. Of course, it's not their fault, but their predecessors'. They haven't prepared any confirmation candidates yet – if they stay it will probably get straightened out in time, since they're both Kelham men. The shape of the church (being round) leads to some queer doings when they turn east for the creed, some folks standing NE, NNE or NE by E, others SE, SSE or SE by E!! Anyway it gave me an awful headache, which hasn't gone properly all day.

It is one of only a handful of circular churches in the country, and was apparently built to this plan by chance. The architect, George Steuart, presented the committee with four possible designs, one rectangular and three circular. The committee chose the rectangular design, but, owing to poor minute-taking, the wrong one was built!

I returned to the Abbey to find the choirmen all discussing where to go for the outing, and the boys (the dear boys!!) holding a meeting of their own in the north porch, with some hope, however vague, of affecting the ultimate decision! Preached again @ P.H. The Bp of Guiana was at the Abbey, but didn't come to supper. They more than doubled the collection, for him to have half.

Monday 18th July

Today he went to Walsall, where he spent the next few days:

No masses at the Abbey this week – because of the spring cleaning. Up at Prestfelde I said goodbye to Tomlinson, who is leaving, & saw the chalice & paten they've been given for the chapel. Priestner (HOR) [*Hostel of the Resurrection – the hostel in Leeds where the College of the Resurrection students spent their undergraduate years*] has applied for a temporary job there, but I don't know if Mr Dovey [*the headmaster*] will have him. Frantic packing, & to Walsall, but not till the 3.30. Went round to Ted Everton's – not in – but John who is 10 & getting big has joined S. Paul's choir. [*Ted Everton was an old school friend of FW, who later went back to teach in the junior forms of Queen Mary's Grammar School, and was godfather to his elder son.*] And at S. Paul's, Mr Joseph Yates, a prominent Methodist, is the organist & choirmaster! On my way I called at S. Andrew's.

This was the church where, in 1939, he was to serve his second curacy, and which he had attended in younger days. Fr G E Waldron Johnston, referred to in the next few entries, was the vicar from 1926 to 1953. See also below under 30th November.

I met Mrs Leech – their Lady worker – who is fine. They must be awfully pleased to have her. She looks after the sacristy – everything is now spotless – and makes new things, including some High Mass vestments (gold). She came from S. Giles', Shrewsbury, learned the true religion from Fr Wynn Griffith at Lichfield, & was then taught how to be a "Lady worker" at Birmingham. She has a SS [*Sunday School*] class – & has got 130 [*Added*: OR IS IT 30?] children for the

11 o/c Mass, as well as the children's Mass on Saturday. I believe she goes round the streets asking the kids
"Do you go to S. Andrew's? Why not?" And gets ac-
cused by all the Bethels of stealing the children. But
as she says – they stole them in the first place!

Tuesday 19th July

Mass of the Holy Angels. I served for Fr Johnston,
as the server is new & didn't turn up. Worrapity [*sic*]
I can't go to S. James' Wednesbury. [*But he did – see
entry for 25th, though there may have been another event
the previous day which he missed.*] Tea at Ted's. Fr
Johnston says that Mr Yates is allowed to receive communion at S. Paul's. [*See the previous day's reference.*] Also
that Fr Talbot of Rushall has had Mr Caddy, the
Mellish Rd Methodist preacher, to preach. And some
of the others equally queer, but Fr Foizey & Millington
stand out (with Fr J.) At the time of the Coronation
– United Service – Johnston was the only one to stand
out. [Added:] ALL THIS AT WALSALL IS SUCK-
ING UP TO THE BISHOP.

Wednesday 20th July

Over to Great Barr to see Auntie Daisy, & found her
in great preparations for the wedding. Gellie & John
are going to live with them. [*Gellie – whose name, like
her mother's, was Daisy Shingler – was FW's cousin, and
was due to get married the following Saturday to Johnnie
Holmes*]. Little Norma, next door, is 18 months old,
& is marvellous! They've united the gardens at the back,
& made a tennis lawn...I'm going to "assist" at the

wedding – & went round to find the vicar, but unsuccessfully.

Thursday 21st July

To L.E.W.F.'s in time for coffee – he had gone to Leicester, but an attack of tonsilitis sent him back. [*This was Luke Freeman, who had been ordained priest three years before, and who at this time was a tutor at Lichfield Theological College. His parents evidently still lived at Walsall. In 1950 he was best man at FW's wedding. He eventually retired to Shrewsbury as assistant priest at St Mary's.*] So I stayed nearly all day – he's not in bed. We had a short walk in the Arboretum – still the same as ever – including the "green'us" and the banana plant. [*This park is very close to the house where FW lived from the age of eight; his family had moved across the town while he was a student.*] Tried to phone Great Barr, but couldn't. Met Daphne & the rest of the Longmores – in a car in Lichfield St., stopped for some reason in the middle of the road, bang in the way of all the traffic. So I insisted on their drawing in before talking to 'em – as I came within an inch of a bad accident myself last night, at the end of Bentley Drive [*where his father and stepmother now lived*]. To the Higgins' tonight – staying late. V. pleased to see me. Glad I went, as they'd wondered at my not writing. [*Old friends at Walsall; Mr Higgins had at one time taught FW in a Sunday school class. They were the parents of the future television actor Frank Windsor.*] I hope I get round to Uncle Dess & Auntie Emmy – as she is said to be rather "queer" – had specialists etc. to her, but of no avail.

Friday 22nd July

Missed Mass again (it was @ 7 o/c – no wonder!). Then to see Fr Foizey – passing the Cenotaph on the way. It is now surrounded by some very ugly railings & chains – about which there has been much correspondence in the W.O. [*Walsall Observer*] & much debate in the Town Council. They appeared suddenly – Alderman Forsythe is reported to have said he was "never so took back" in his life, as when his gaze fell on them for the first time. Similarly at Birmingham they have had some nude figures sprung upon them in a public place, which have raised a lot of controversy. The point is that they are men – had they been women, no one wd have minded! If we <u>must</u> cover up our bodies – why not begin on some people's <u>faces</u>?

Outside S. Michael's (which is as it always was) I met Mrs Selby. Then a chat with Fr Foizey, & then to Luke's for lunch. His throat is much worse, but he wouldn't go to bed. Stayed till tea, and then went to inspect the new church at Fullbrook – nearly finished, & <u>very</u> good. Quite big. The housing estate out there is simply VAST! Also saw inside Palfrey Church – it really is lovely, I had no idea. I shd say quite the nicest church in Walsall. And Millington is making it go. Then at 9 o/c a rehearsal for the High Mass @ S. Andrew's. They follow Adrian almost to the letter. It differs much from Mirfield, of course – more particularly in having no Greater Entry, & in having me, subdeacon, standing from the Offertory to the Paternoster with the Paten under the Humeral veil. Quite as pointless as the Greater Entry!

This use of the humeral veil appears to go back to the eighth century. The Greater Entry is the name for the solemn procession at which the bread and the wine are carried to the altar. "Adrian" refers to Adrian Fortescue, *The ceremonies of the Roman rite described* (1919) revised by J B O'Connell (1930), a widely-used directory of ceremonial practice, much used by Anglo-Catholics at this period.

The Worsull [*sic*] accents of the M.C. [*Master of Ceremonies – a role in High Mass filled by a layman*] and servers were very rich! The new curate, Fr Riley, is a good fellow, & at Caldmore Fr F said the same of his new curate.

Saturday 23rd July

The day of the wedding.

Mass 9.15. Shopping & coffee (about a dozen children, Mrs Leech & Fr Riley). To Great Barr, arriving at S Margaret's Church about 2. Again, no one at the rectory. The Verger volunteered the information that the Vicar of Streetly [*Edward Hooton, ordained priest 1903*] was coming – & he did, just on time. He walked up the drive behind the bride (but she was early). Norman (best man) & Johnnie (looking even younger than his 21 years) were very early indeed. The priest was very old (61) but very nice, & said the usual "few words" afterwards practically by heart – but no one realised it. I said the beginning & the end, leaving out the verbose bits of the last prayer. [*"Hear what the holy Scripture doth say as touching the duty of husbands towards their wives, and wives towards their husbands." It goes on for over two pages!*] I didn't want to omit the reasons why matrimony was ordained, but he whispered to me, so I did! [*"For the procreation of children, ...for a remedy against sin, ...for the mutual society, help and comfort that the one ought to have of the other".*] Gellie looked lovely, & there was quite a large crowd. About 35 or so to "tea" afterwards. Being a really lovely day, we were able to have it on the lawn – but it was if anything a bit too hot. Met Sister Whitty, & the Doc, & his dispenser, Maurice...

Came away just after 7, & called at Sandwell St. to break the news. Unfortunately Nancy was on holidays (hiking). [*Another branch of the Shingler family. It is not obvious why they were not at the wedding. They kept an off-license at 2, Sandwell Street. Nancy's father, Alfred, had played football for Walsall.*] They really have done a terrific lot of slum clearance in Walsall, including this neighbourhood (Church Hill). On arriving home I found a parcel from Mrs Lloyd, including among other things a p.c. from A.D. on his holidays, God bless him. And from Walsingham I hear I shall have to be put up in the village. Hope it doesn't mean there's a pilgrimage on. [*See below on 26th July.*]

Johnnie has 4 elder brothers, who all resemble him remarkably!

Sunday, Trinity V, 1938

Assisted with the chalice at S. Andrew's, 8 o/c. Bernard [*Johnston, the vicar's son*] had to receive communion standing (broken kneecap, getting better). There one can wear cassock & biretta through the streets without causing anyone to stare! Back again at 11 o/c, to be subdeacon. This went off very well & was a great joy. The new vestments are most beautiful. The SS boy (Green?) whom I palled up with 12 months ago has become a server – having grow'd out of knowledge, like our Harry. [*FW's youngest brother, then aged fifteen.*] Cup o'tea with the curate (Riley) & chat – he came from Sunderland & knows Fr Bill – says his work there hasn't lasted – the people only go when he goes back – when of course he tells them off roundly – but the wretched folks merely say "what a nice sermon!!" Grr! And when one thinks of him breaking down, etc. ...

[*Added at top of this page:* Ora pro [*Pray for*] B. & A.J.]

Arranged to call for Bernard to morrow, if the doc says he can, to go to Wedy. [*Wednesbury*] Then, by Fr J's car, to S. George's. Here I found the catechism class, very small indeed, only boys, being taken by Mr Cookson. [*Organist and choirmaster at S. George's, Walsall, a post he held until the church was closed in 1965.*] He was "explaining" the BCP to them. His interpretations were partly amusing & partly, in such a church, tragic. To make oneself thoroughly happy about the Abbey, it is only necessary to visit S. George's. The Vicar turned up, & with him I visited the SS. Numbers about 60. Frances Porteen & Daphne's sister, & Miss Cottam & a few others, plus a number of strangers. Frances is getting married quite soon (her sailor boy). Tea at the Vicarage (he claims to stand side by side with Fr Johnston, the only other, in the dispute about the Nonconformists).

[*Added at top of this page:* Write to F.P]

Preached at Evensong – the same sermon – about catching men, as at S. Andrew's (& S. Chad's & our P.H.). [*Presumably on Mark 1.16-20, for St James, whose festival was the next day.*] They were only small, & S.G's has the worst echo of any church I've yet spoken or read in. It was an unexpectedly happy experience. The old faces. The old choir. Charlie Badger, Ralph Daley, Ernie, Mr Hubball, etc. & the top boys who were there when I was a choirman. Leonard Nock, whose voice has gone, was still there, till the outing, & making an awful piercing noise! Harry [*his brother*], had he stayed, wd certainly have left by now! Last week they were looked after by an ex-Army chaplain, who gave the boys toffees to eat during the sermon, & preached about slate pencils or sumpn [*sic*]. Then afterwards they came up & inquired if I, even I, wd be coming next week! (I mean the boys did.) [*The construction "I, even I" is a humorous echo of the 1611 translation of I Kings, ch. 19, v. 10.*]

Supper with Mr & Mrs Cookson. It has been a great treat, seeing all the old familiar faces, but oh, so tiring. Back in the Cookson's car. He will be retiring from dayschool, soon. At S. Andrew's, I preached in biretta. Ted came. We had lace albs – in which I was not altogether happy! Mrs J [*Johnston – the Vicar's wife*] has a pet phrase, for when hearing of tragic news – "Oh how thankful we ought to be!" Remember it. It came out funnily – but she told us of a poor child who caught leprosy from a banana skin. I hadn't remembered what a Lido the canal at Birchills becomes in the summer – crowded with swimmers – very few indeed in costumes.

Monday 25th July

Didn't open my eyes till 10 o/c – therefore no mass! Packed. Then to get a cycle ticket, where the man mistook me for a papist. Told me he'd read about Walsingham in the *Catholic Herald*. At the Freeman's, Luke not yet better. Then tea at the Everton's, where Mrs E is not as "queer" as they all said. [*In this context, this means "ill"*]. Evening to S. James', Wednesbury, calling for Bernard Johnston, who is now able to walk with only one stick. [*This would have been for the patronal festival, St James' Day.*] Fr Ravizotti was on the same bus, & also J.O. from Wood Green, both with servers. Glad to see J.O. there! They have made a wonderful transformation at S. James' – now a really beautiful church. There were 10 or a dozen priests in the open-air procession, & a crowd of servers. The Salvation Army band, many banners, much incense, & a Guild of Our Lady in white. Also CLB boys. [*Church Lads' Brigade.*] Neither Frs E.F [*Edgar Foizey*] nor W.H [*William Hassall*] were there, but Fr W.E. [*Wilfrid Ellis*] was, & Frs Millington & Johnston were deacons of honour to Bp. Roscow Shedden. [*A former Bishop of Nassau, 1919-1931, now retired as Vicar of Wantage.*] I walked (behind J.O. & before W.E.) next to the future vicar of Ronald Redfern. It was typical Black Country, except where slum clearance had made such a difference. We sang *Jerusalem my happy home!*, *For all the Saints*, & another hymn, & then began again. [*Added*: Sometimes the band played too many verses

& sometimes not enough!! It was <u>NOT</u> the S.A.] Back in church a 10 minute sermon, & Devotions in a manner authorised by the Bp, i.e. without a Benediction & without censing the B.S., & altered antiphon. [*Benediction is a service of blessing the people in which the Reserved Sacrament is displayed in the monstrance. The Oxford Dictionary of the Christian Church says that in the C of E it "is forbidden in some dioceses, allowed in modified form (as 'Adoration' or 'Devotions') in others, and in a few...encouraged".*] The congregation (packed) sang wonderfully. Harold Jones, a server from S. Andrews, sat next to me and the priests. Bernard & I were invited in to the clergy house afterwards. Sherry & a cigarette. Bus back, but we had to walk up to Birchills.

Tuesday 26th July

Departure 8.30, changed Birmingham & Fakenham only, arrived Walsingham 2.40 and a nice cup of tea! Everything here is marvellous – the completed church is v. fine. And now there is a scheme for a priests' college, to look after the shrine, retreatants, etc. The sister in charge (Grace Helen, S.S.P.) explained how they are the original Horbury Sisters, the remnant being S. Peter's Chains. In the old days the Mirfield students used to hike over on saints' days for tea & vespers at Horbury. She knew Fr Symonds very well. On the lawn was Fr Bristow (surprisingly like Fr H.B. in appearance), [*curate*] of S. Chad's, Longton. Besides him there were only a lot of females, until Reynolds, the M.C. last night at W'bury, turned up. Bristow is in my old room, 'neath the creaking sign, but I am bedded out at the

Page's in the village. Notice the Roman Franciscans who have descended upon the place. They have turned a couple of houses into a hostel, and have bought a row of houses where they will build a church when the lease is up.

At Walsingham in Norfolk, the mediaeval cult of the Holy House at Nazareth had been revived in recent years. In 1931 the reconstructed Holy House (originally built in the eleventh century, traditionally on the instructions of Our Lady herself) was opened. In 1934 the Slipper Chapel (one and a half miles away) was opened as a rival Roman Catholic shrine. Fr Hope Patten, Vicar of Walsingham and the Administrator at the (Anglican) Shrine, commented drily: "The conditions are not unlike those in the Holy Land where the Orthodox and the Latins, the Armenians and other Easterns, all claim the Holy Sites and live together, treading on each other's toes more or less frequently."

The College of St Augustine, referred to above, was a long-standing project of Hope Patten, which never really succeeded; by 1955 there had been sixteen members, of whom five had remained attached to the foundation under renewable three-year vows.

The Community of St Peter's Chains at Horbury, Yorkshire, had sent nuns to run a hospice for pilgrims since early in Patten's time.

FW's books included a guide to the shrine, inscribed O.L.W. GRATIAS 1938.

Wednesday 27th July

Served Bristow at Mass in the Holy House itself. Then he had to go. Fr Derek Lingwood took him as far as

Fakenham, & I went with them. [*Derrick Lingwood was Patten's 'right-hand man', acting as bursar and a Guardian of the Shrine.*] In the Abbey grounds with Reynolds before lunch, EXPECTANS DUM DEFLUAT AMNIS [*waiting till the rain stopped*], & afterwards to Sandringham Flower Show – which was all very nice but very tiring. [*The Latin is an adapted quotation from Horace – Rusticus expectat dum defluat amnis – the country bumpkin waits till the river stops flowing. Ep. I.ii.32.*] The church there extremely disappointing, queer altar. [*Rebuilt by William Cobbes in the sixteenth century, and restored by Lady Harriet Cowper shortly before the estate was purchased by Prince Albert. This is, of course, the royal family's parish church, and, while FW was no republican, his churchmanship will have diverged significantly from that of George VI and Queen Elizabeth. The flamboyant silver altar, which was given in memory of Edward VII and dedicated in 1911, is described in some quarters as "magnificent" – it is evidently distinctive.*]

Thursday 28th July

A jolly sight harder to get up today. Mr Page is a cheery little fat man, who expects to hold a prolonged conversation about the weather at 7 o/c a.m. – and to find out where I've been the day before! Mass in the Parish Church. About 20 present, including the fellow who served last year. A funny little server today, with a piping voice & a local accent. There was noise at the back like a decrepit steam roller making its way up the aisle, & in came the proprietress of the Martyr café. She then sat down & coughed as though about to pass out, but in the middle of the morning she was

dressed up to kill and doing 60 down the road, off &
away somewhere.

In the afternoon by bike to South Creake, where is
England's most beautiful church. 4 altars, including
Nave Altar, Reservation, statues, peal of bells, old
woodwork – & no pews. A few chairs brought out for
the service suffice for the whole population of the
village. [*Added*: BEAUTIFULLY CLEAN.] Some of
the others came by car. [*Added*: IE MRS & MISS
DANIELS AND "MONICA".] Others walked.

We were back for tea – those who walked were NOT.
There was a spare seat in the car – after all my exertions
getting the bike here, I might just as well have left it
behind!

The Church of St Mary, South Creake, three miles from
Walsingham, is mediaeval, with angels on the hammer-beam
roof added to celebrate the battle of Agincourt. The rood screen
and pulpit are early fifteenth century. It still maintains an
Anglo-Catholic tradition, established by Fr Charles Hepworth
in 1921. Simon Jenkins in *England's Hundred Best Churches*
says "The cumulative impact of South Creake is of a richly
endowed place of worship as it might have been before the
Reformation cleared it of colour and clutter", so it is not
surprising that FW liked it!

This morning the cubs who were at Mass the other
day were being shown round the shrine. They have two
cubmistresses, one of whom [*Added*: (A)] is <u>most</u>
attractive. They are from Kenton (London) & their
priest [*Frank Johnson, Vicar of St Mary the Virgin,*

Kenton, Middlesex] knew Sidney Cockburn [*a student at the College, a year behind FW and so about to be ordained deacon*]. The cubmistresses came to the Hospice after dinner too.

The cubs and their 'most attractive' cubmistress, who plays a significant part in this diary, were from Kenton, in the Harrow area, which had become an independent parish with the expansion of the suburbs of London. It had had a permanent church, St Mary's, only as recently as 1936. An attempt in 2003 to trace the cubmistress, Audrey, was unsuccessful, despite the kind assistance of the present vicar and of a former inhabitant who joined the cubs – under a different 'Akela' – in 1943. After so many years, we cannot be surprised. It should be added that neither of FW's sons remember him mentioning her at any time.

Friday 29th July, S. Martha

This afternoon to the cubs' camp for tea – a very jolly time. Fr Taylor, Fr Edwards: two awfully nice men; Audrey & somebody else: & 20 boys. After tea & bread an' marmalade (+ 2 cakes which a lady in the village brought round warm from the oven), some of us went fishing. The boys had dug for worms with a spade as big as themselves, & we fastened one to a hook in a most gruesome manner. Needless to say, we caught nothing, but we saw a lot of dace, some moorhens & some nests, & got well stung with nettles. Johnny Creame became Red Wolf, an o[ther?] White Feathers, & I Black Beetle because of my blazer. Johnnie knew all about the Lamb of God on my badge. [*The symbol of the Community and College of the Resurrection.*] At dinner there was another man – from Brighton. At the weekend some of us are going to make a proper pilgrimage, & I am to conduct Stations of the Cross. In the drawing room a musical lady tried to pick out the Walsingham Hymn on the piano – from the musical statue & our singing! A short walk round by the church, & so to bed at 10.30.

Saturday 30th July

Sung Mass at the Parish Church (8 o/c). They sing the Saturday Mass of Our Lady every Saturday in the side chapel. Incense. One server. Reynolds departed, among general regret, to catch the one o/c train to Wednesbury (Awful thought). Afternoon I spent with the cubs, it was their sports, & a gorgeously hot day. Little Johnnie didn't run much – the sun affected him, so we laid him in the shade, & I wet my hankie in the brook & he loved to have it on his forehead. He's not a strong boy, & Miss Daniels thinks he won't live long. She's had experience & says she can tell. He fainted at mass in the parish church last Sunday – just after the Consecration – unwittingly preventing the Kensitites from making a disturbance. He has a brother, but no sisters, and "no animals". [*Added, apparently with reference to the treatment of Johnnie:*] Audrey was magnifique!

For the Kensitites, see above, 7th July.

At 5.45 we began our pilgrimage with devotions in the Holy House before the usual intercessions – conducted by Fr Patten himself. There were a lot of newcomers arrived. At 7 o/c a whole crowd made their confessions – Fr Patten merely said to me "Have you got a regular director?" So I said "Yes" – "Anything you wish to ask about?" – "No" – & that was all. After supper, we went to the cubs Camp Fire singsong, & Mrs Daniels presented the prizes for the sports. It was most excellently jolly. And now it's far too hot to sleep. At dinner I told Mrs D. that I always spoil it for myself by wondering what they will be like in 20 years time – & she said, very kindly & quietly, "You mustn't wonder."

Mem. Don't wonder, just thank God & worship the Christ child in them.

Lady, help of Christians, pray for us.

Sunday 31st July '38

By the way – what a number of people with monocles I've suddenly begun meeting – first the doctor at Great Barr – then the priest at Wednesbury – then Mrs Brett, I see, has one for reading! When wearing her veil and smoking, she looks just like a gipsy.

Mass & Communion at 8 this morning. At 10 o/c I conducted Stations – cotta & purple stole [*a cotta is a short surplice. For the stole see below under 1st October.*] – it was all very good. Audrey says Fr Taylor didn't let any of the cubs go into the Sepulchre. Just as well! [*In the garden at Walsingham is a model of the Empty Tomb.*] Then the Parish Mass at the church – absolutely packed. Again a great joy. The devotion (as Reynolds said) could be cut with a spade. It was wonderful. Local people too – not by any means all visitors. And Fr Patten preached a delightful sermon. Asperged first. The cubs & their officers all came. I sat behind them. Johnnie turned round – he says he wants to keep my hanky. Podgy Tucker looked as tho' about to faint, but it turned out he was only asleep!

I pointed out to some of them the Abbey ruins – they hadn't been in owing to the price (6d). They will go back to school with new ideas of Henry VIII – what with me & Fr Derek! Mrs & Miss Daniels are going to give me a copy of *The House of Prayer* which belonged to their granny (cp Fr Biggart reading it in my first retreat). [*And indeed they did, as will be seen below! As for Henry VIII, no one influenced by FW could ever have a good opinion of him!*]

At 2.15 Fr Patten gave us a short talk in S. Anne's chapel – new idea – the Lady of the Manor. [*Presumably a talk about Richeldis, the lady of the manor, who in 1061 had a vision which led to her building the original Holy House.*] Then we sang Litany of Our Lady in procession & were sprinkled etc. at the Holy Well. I helped with the devotions, & again all was excellent. At Evensong – no sermon, but Benediction afterwards – as one would expect, great devotion, driving one back to realities. On the way back we said goodbye to the cubs. I shook hands scoutwise [*i.e. left-handed*] with each one.

Tomorrow I shall get to Mass after all, as there is an early one. Then Miss D will take me to Fakenham in the car (if it don't break down) & thus avoid the hour's wait at Fakenham. [*This was to take FW on to the scout camp at Kelham for the second part of his holiday.*]

Audrey came round after supper (purposely not bringing Geoffrey, tho' he was invited!) & we talked till nearly 11 o/c! Outside the "Martyrs' memorial" I borrowed 5/- from Mr Williams, who keeps the Shrine Token Shop. Audrey, you see, is not only a magnificent girl, but also a good Catholic. At intercessions I gave in several: choirboys, Fr W's neuritis, & D.P.'s TB. Furthermore, I shall not forget my Pilgrimage Intention – it is already being answered.

PS Fr Hope Patten's theology was absolutely sound this afternoon. Audrey's birthday is 20th November.

Monday 1st August

Mass & Communion @ 7.30, a crowd of people besides the cubs. Audrey & Geoffrey & Fr Edwards too. The Mass was said by Fr Taylor. Johnny was at the back, but after a bit I looked down & there he was by my side! What must be passing through his little head! I gave him the pad from my kneeling chair – it wd have been screwmaticy for his knees on the stones. White Feathers was just in front. They both said goodbye again at the end of Mass. Did I mention White Feathers? I was Black Beetle (because of my blazer, belt and shoes) and Johnny varied – but finally decided on Red Wolf.

A quick breakfast, & by car to Fakenham, with a W'ham label on my bag. The journey wasn't bad, in spite of being Bank Holiday – met two batches of nice people. At Spalding I had a walk round the town (a 2 hours wait). Arrived Gainsborough in time for tea & to help get ready with the packing. Great confusion when the train arrived unexpectedly at G'boro', & I was half undressed and asleep owing to the great heat!! The boys here are quite nice, but not outstanding! Pete on the parallel bars was best – they are on the whole a bit cheeky to Bertie. [*Bertie Jones, FW's old college friend. See above under 7th July.*] Still, he gets on a whole lot better than some people, who didn't understand, would have expected. Sleeping tonight at a house opposite his digs. [*Added:*] Don't think much of his church! Couldn't stand it. Thoughts of Audrey.

Bertie had been ordained deacon in 1936 and priest in 1937. He was at this time curate at Holy Trinity, Gainsborough, where he "ran a scout troop, started afresh from the wreckage of one that collapsed after the previous curate left; not because of any special qualification on my part...but because no one else would take it on." In his parish magazine column in 1977 he recalled his memories of this summer camp. "We had daily Mass in camp... . A former fellow student at Mirfield, a year junior and at that time a deacon came and helped me run the camp...with very happy results. [This] camp was in the grounds of Kelham, then, I suppose, in its hey-day... . This was only a few weeks before my final departure from Gainsborough in [September] 1938, and, for me at least, the thought of parting so soon cast an occasional shadow over a very happy week." [*In a large room*, No. 5. *Magazine of St Alban's, Ilford*, 1977.] In a later article he added: "To my dismay and indignation, it was treated as a week of my holiday. Holiday, indeed! If anything it ought to have qualified me for an extra week off to recuperate."[*In a large room*, No. 7.]

The church, which FW didn't "think much of" was built in 1842, and is described by Bertie as "certainly one of the ugliest and [most] inconvenient I have ever known". The ground-plan "had three arms [of the cross-shape] the same length and very narrow, thus not only wasting a lot of ground but ensuring that only a third of the seats had a front view of the High Altar... . Two thirds of the congregation could not see the other third." The altar steps were so narrow that it was impossible to stand on either of the lower steps, and even on the top step "the celebrant had to beware of falling off. The fittings and decorations were incredibly and depressingly ugly." [*In a large room*, No. 3.]

Tuesday 2nd August

Mattins 7 – Mass 7.30, with a number of the boys present. It was said by Fr Florey, the Vicar, who is a Burmese. [*He had come to England to train for ordination in 1914, and was eventually ordained after distinguished war service. Bertie describes him as "very pleasant and friendly...highly regarded by most of those who attended his church and by many more who did not." He appears however to have been insufficiently "high" for the two young curates. In a large room, No.2,6,9.*] After breakfast, bought plimsolls for use in camp, & then helped load the lorry, & so to Kelham by road.

A good camp site at end of cricket field. In passing the House we noticed that the students were still up – tho' it is August week! Later, to the Kitchen for milk & bread. Note how they do all their own housework. Somebody dropped a cake into a huge vat of tea, & merely said "Sorry" & there were no comments. 'Twould not have been so at Mirfield. Owing to their clockwork system it was imposs to get anything till 3.30, so I took the two boys to see the chapel. Fearfully good – just what I like – stark & simple – wonderful Rood – but only five altars. There will be more when it is finished, & they hope to start some more building soon.

Kelham was another Anglo-Catholic theological college, run by the Society of the Sacred Mission. It was based on a Victorian Gothic mansion designed by Gilbert Scott. For more on the architecture, see below under 4th August. According to the SSM: "The Great Chapel was dedicated in 1928 and was a masterpiece. It was almost square with a great central dome, (62 feet across and 68 feet high) the second largest concrete dome in England. A few visitors said it reminded them of Stonehenge – massive, austere and mysterious." The rood is life-size, with the figures of Christ, St Mary and St John, and was completed in 1929, the work of Sergent Jagger. When Kelham closed in 1973 and the SSM moved to Willen Priory, Milton Keynes, the rood was brought there also, where it may now be seen in the garden.

Sharing tent (a new one) with Leonard Cuthbert, not a scout. The boys' names are Peter Denton, Peter Wilsey, Bernard (Mick) Walker, Alan ("Fat") Spicksley, Walter Slaton, & Sidney. 3 in a patrol, so that the meals are done quicker & they all have a turn.

Wednesday 3rd August

Mass in church tent – very good altar, complete with stone, plus the usual ornaments & cards, & a lady statue. Visits from the students, esp. Walls (an old Sandonian, school pal of Bertie's [*from Sandown Grammar School, in the Isle of Wight*]) & his friend from Cumberland. Walls wanted to come to Mass on S. Dominic's day [*4th August*] (his patron, and actually not kept at Kelham!) but cdn't get permission from his chaplain (a kind of tutor-cum-spiritual director). [*Roland Walls was ordained priest in 1941; in 1948 he returned to Kelham as a lecturer.*] Bathing this afternoon in the river – rather a strong current, & dangerous pot-holes, left by the army in the war-time after making a pontoon bridge. [*Kelham Hall was used by the military during the First World War.*] We wear further up where some cows were, & found it better. Bertie's middle protrudes in the most awful manner!

Thursday 4th August

Much rain early this morning – & ours is a leaking tent. Apparently all new tents leak until they've got thoroughly wetted! Fortunately the breakfast was only eggs. The boys are surprisingly good cooks, & we aren't allowed to help them!

At 10.30 we were <u>all</u> taken round the House & church by Walls & his friend. Tho' they are still up, it was only for exams, & these are nearly all over, so they are free. Cricket & tennis every afternoon. The House (in the old part) is a far worse example of Victorian vulgarity than anything I've ever seen. The Mirfield house may be "the acme of Victorian domesticity" – but this is all gilded & decorated like the structures on a fair ground. The students & laybrethren are tackling the problem by painting it all over during the vacs, but it has been endured for nearly 50 years! The new parts of the house are very good indeed, & I received an invitation to use the τοποι instead of the scouts' latrines – but I declined the bathroom with thanks! 'Twouldn't be camping!

Into Southwell this afternoon, where we saw the Minster & what we took to be the Bishop's Palace. This was confirmed by the Bp coming out later & speaking to us. [*Henry Mosley, Bishop of Southwell since 1928.*] Up the Tower – but Bernard & Sidney didn't enjoy the heights! At the top the verger inquired about Kenneth Wright, who used to be a choirboy here. [*At the College of the Resurrection 1937, ordained priest 1940.*] We attended Evensong as far as the end of the Psalms. They were sung according to the most modern system of pointing, & of course the people made no effort at all to join in. It really is impossible, tho' they are supposed to be congregational. As a musical rendering however, they were very good, & the 22nd Psalm was most moving. [*"My God, my God, look upon me; why hast thou forsaken me?" It is the psalm particularly associated with the events of Good Friday.*]

A dreadfully hot day. In a sweetshop the woman asked if we were from the monastery – strange that Mirfield is never so called. I suppose t'Resurrection is easier! No sooner had we got back than we espied Fr Antony Selwyn arriving by bike. He stayed the night, bringing his own tent ("a day's march nearer home"). Last year he spent the whole time with them, & was a great favourite. A commissioner turned up to tea – not however the one, but merely a visitor. He said of

Staffordshire that it was "a bonny part of the country to be proud of".

Father Selwyn was a member of the Community of the Resurrection. "A day's march nearer home" is a quotation from a sentimental Victorian hymn, not often sung nowadays, but certainly in the editions of *Hymns Ancient & Modern* and the *English Hymnal* that were in print in 1938.

> 'For ever with the Lord!'
> Amen; so let it be;
> Life from the dead is in that word,
> 'Tis immortality.
> Here in the body pent,
> Absent from him I roam,
> Yet nightly pitch my moving tent
> A day's march nearer home.

Camp Fire tonight. Fr Selwyn told a story – about S. Oswald (tomorrow) [*the great Christian king of Northumbria, killed in battle against the pagan king Penda, 5th August 642*], and a number of students dropped in, but they had to be away dead on time for Compline. [*The last service of the day.*] We had a very good sing indeed with their help. Most of them were "cottagers" – not allowed to smoke till they leave the cottage at nineteen. Mckee & Tranter specially pally.

Friday 5th August

In to Newark this afternoon. The open-air bath very good – blue tiles on bottom. At the Parish Church (not bad at all) we went <u>down</u> the crypt, much to the relief of Bernard & Sidney, who pointed to the spire as we drew near & said "Well, at any rate we ain't going up there!"

They cooked excellent omelettes for breakfast, & marvellous vegetable stew, & in Newark we ordered sausages and Sunday joint. Leonard & I went to Evensong at the ch, & I met Bill Hopkinson for a few moments, who has been ill & unable to get across to the camp. But he looked well, & is actually getting plump! Mckee & Tranter came & talked a lot, comparing Kelham & Mirfield etc.; they all seem to think we have a very good time! At the same time we got on to the subject of Confession, & it will probably result in Len's making his first.

Saturday 6th August

Len & I waved off those students whom we knew at 8.20 (after Mass & before breakfast). A nasty wet morning. We seem to be having the edge of a pretty general & bad Thunderstorm. Mckee had a box of fat cigarettes (greys) which he intends to start on as soon as they reach the station @ Newark! It appears this was why Norman Gilmore left Kelham! [*Norman Gilmore was at the College of the Resurrection in 1938, and was ordained priest in 1941.*]

At lunch, first of all the genuine Commissioner turned up & inspected us, & then a very fine person – one Roy Blythe. Only 17, but so well developed you'd think he was 21. A first class scout & regular communicant. Immediately after lunch I was stung by putting my arm down on a wasp, & he sucked the sting etc. out immediately. Yesterday Bernard Walker was badly stung – tried to climb a tree which had a wasps' nest at the foot of it – came out hitting himself in the face & yelling like mad! Would that I had been there to see!

Also I forgot to mention that Fr Selwyn told us a little of the passing of Bp Frere. How he came slowly up to the House after lecturing to the College; couldn't eat anything, and said quietly, "Well, I think this is the end" and it was. Quite ready.

In the Easter 1938 issue of *The Mirfield Gazette*, p. 3, Thomas Hannay recorded of Frere:

He has during this year lectured in Church History with all his old ease and sparkle, with his amazing power to sum up vividly and acutely a situation, a movement or a person's character in an unforgettable sentence.... . He was gifted beyond the measure of most men, and not a gift was wasted, but was used to the full in unremitting toil. He has passed to the rest he has earned: in his father's hands we leave him.

FW continued:

In the afternoon we had the boat out on the river – no oars & no sail, so we used a good stout rope & went a long way before being hauled back. Also as I wore my plimsolls in the water it was more comfortable, & only a little more difficult in swimming.

Then the fond mothers & relations of the boys arrived, together with Fr Florey, it being Visitors' Day. They were immediately taken down to the river, while I re-lit both fires to boil the tea. Everything else was ready, including a salad which had been dropped in the grass by Bertie himself, & very carefully picked up. Roy & the others did the honours – I found I couldn't stand their inane remarks. Not having seen <u>any women at all</u>, all the week, it was quite queer. Only one woman in a million should be allowed anywhere near a camp – & at the moment that one is of course named Audrey. And she is <u>not</u> a guide. Strange how most scouts don't think much of Guides! When the boys commented that I didn't look bad in my cassock (Bertie's being very disreputable), I told them that somebody else had said so too, & this led to much laughter later on at Bernard's remark about "Fr Wain's matched!" – & Bertie's puzzlement. Strange how I quickly became Father Wain, while he remained Mr Jones, but I daresay it would be the same with Abbey boys, were the positions reversed… . Camp Fire tonight again – the students being gone we had only "Novice Banning" as a guest, & I told a story ("The old man who lived in a churchyard"). Unfortunately the fire took some time to get going. The novice came in time for cocoa & biscuits, after rounding up the sheep they keep here, with the aid of some of the boys. They also keep pigs. Roy invited me to share his tent, to avoid my leaking one (Len having gone today with the visitors) & also so that we could watch the campfire through the door. Lying there watching it, & smoking cigarettes. Also lying awake next morning listening to all manner of birds' cries.

The story FW told might have been *There was a Man Dwelt by a Churchyard* – a ghost story by M R James first published in book form in 1931.

Sunday, Trinity VIII 1938

There should have been an A.R.P. [*Air Raid Precautions*] "Black out" last night, with 700 aeroplanes – but it didn't come off, as 5 pilots were killed when taking off in the mist.

I was stung again today, by putting my hand on a wasp again. Took Roy round the church as he didn't see it properly with the visitors' tour yesterday. He understood about Reservation, since he comes, not from Holy Trinity, but S. John's, Gainsborough. Here they reserve in an aumbry in an upstairs chapel. [*A cupboard, originally for sacred vessels and books, commonly nowadays for the Reserved sacrament.*] Also they have a Lady Chapel in the House itself, but no statue!

Preached at Evensong at Kelham Parish Church – with the scouts we made a good-sized congregation. "Another point off for Fr Wain, laughing in church!" – because I smiled at them. The people have a right of way through the grounds to their church, & the Rector (who was present) thought it such a good idea for them to hear a strange voice! ("Come" – as at Prestfelde & the Abbey). [*Presumably a reference to his text.*] While the church bells were ringing (they have three), the boys, all dressed up in readiness, were getting hot & bothered chasing the S.S.M. pigs, who had escaped! The vestry is in a different style from the rest of the church – a horrible ballroom type, with a huge effigy of a man & his wife occupying nearly all of the floor space. It was probably built specially for them! Then while we were impatient to get back to camp

& supper, the aged Rector kept us over 20 mins. talking about Norway & Switzerland.

St Wilfred's, Kelham, is a sixteenth-century church, renovated in 1844. "Here is a richly wrought monument of the last Lord Lexington and his Lady, of fine statuary marble, but the figures are strangely placed back-to-back." – so said *White's Directory of Nottinghamshire, 1853.*

Monday 8th August

Roy departed at 6.0 this morning, to get back to work at Gainsborough. The alarm went off at the unearthly hour of 5, & if I hadn't woken him again at 5.30, there'd have been an unholy rush. We shared my tent, so that he could pack his in readiness. It rained in a little in the small hours.

A slack day – except for a long trudge round Newark to interview the stationmaster about my journey tomorrow. Fortunately they had saved me some tea (radishes & cake). Bro. Edgar at the SSM had thought it imposs to make use of my return tickets. I shall have to reclaim on the Gainsborough-Spalding one, but can use the other, & only have to take a single to Leicester, not Birmingham.

A last Camp Fire – very good. Novice Banning came back after Compline, & told a story – A good fire, fortunately.

Tuesday 9th August

Helped to pack for a while, & then many goodbyes
("It may be for years & it may be for ever").

The allusion is to the old Irish ballad, *Kathleen Mavourneen*,
composed by Frederick William Nicholls Crouch.

Oh, hast thou forgotten how soon we must sever,
Oh, hast thou forgotten this day we must part?
It may be for years and it may be forever,
Then why art thou silent, thou voice of my heart?

This was popular at the time of the American Civil War and
was certainly the sort of song that might have been sung
around the scouts' campfire.

Bus into Newark to catch the 11.14, no change to
Birmingham. But it was 5/6 to Leicester, & I'd only
4/11, so the clerk lent me 7d. He did it with a bad
grace, I'm afraid, as he thought he was being diddled,
but it was good of him all the same. And in my bag
the bottle of aftershaving lotion leaked over the cover
of my office book. [*A book containing the services for
fixed hours of the day, Mattins, Lauds, Prime, Terce, Sext,
None, Vespers and Compline.*] Then there was the gap
from Birmingham to Wolverhampton to be bridged,
as I'd only a return from Wolverhampton to Shrewsbury.
So I had to see the station-master's clerk at New Street,
& prove my identity. He too thought he was being
diddled (it happens a lot), but when he realised I was
genuine, he became kindness itself. In Shrewsbury I
first met Bilcliffe – then Mrs Vaughan!! Who told me

all the news, especially the deaths. "Aunty Polly" has died unexpectedly at the Woodnorth's. Out to Evensong I met Tony, then afterwards the Woodnorth boys. The house (53) is being partly re-painted – "Good!" as Bernard wd have said. A jolly good hot bath, & very thankful. [*This refers to 53, Abbey Foregate, where he had digs.*]

Wednesday 10th August

Much letterwriting. And my cheque – hooray! And the Vicar has lots of visiting in store for me, of the house-to-house variety. Saw Anna Neagle in *Victoria the Great* at the Granada – very good.

This film had been made the previous year, marking the centenary of the accession of Queen Victoria. It had scenes shot at real royal palaces and using genuine royal carriages. Neagle was directed by Herbert Wilcox, whom she later married. Her co-star was Anton Walbrook.

"The nights are drawing in, & the Gaumont British News wishes to be the first to tell you so." Mrs Lloyd was the second, when she brought my supper. The Mission church is not yet started on, for some reason.

This was the church of St Peter's, Monkmoor, which was eventually consecrated in March 1939. It was a mission church within the parish of the Abbey in the growing suburbs of Shrewsbury.

From now on, I shall try, however unsuccessfully, to record as little as possible in this diary. It surely ought to be enough merely for holidays & big events – eg ordination, for which the *Si Quis* forms have arrived. But I've not YET got a license to preach!

Si Quis forms are the notices issued on behalf of an ordinand, inviting objections.

Saturday 13th August

Very difficult to settle down after the holiday. But it's a good place to come back to, better than some! So here's to. The Daniels (Mrs & Miss) have sent "Timothy" – jolly good.

This book, which survives amongst FW's, is actually called *The House of Prayer*, and is by Florence Converse, published Dent, 1924. For the previous references to it, see above, July 31st. The copy is inscribed, firstly, "To dearest mum with Nan's love, Aug 1926", and then (in FW's writing) "FROM MRS & MISS DANIEL IN MEMORY OF A WEEK AT WALSINGHAM JULY 1938, NOT FORGETTING MY FIRST RETREAT". It is a curious book – the fictionalised story of a child's learning about the Christian faith and church history, a blend of religious sentimentality and (not entirely unconscious) humour. Perhaps the best sample of the latter is given by the following exchange:

"Timothy," said grandfather, peering over his spectacles at the books on the floor, "is that my prayer-book of Edward VI, flapping its precious pages in the evening breeze, on those dusty boards?"

"No, sir; it's only the Ante-Nicene Liturgies translated from the originals by J M Neale."

Inside this book was a covering letter from Mary Daniel at 279, Wightman Road, Hornsey, dated 11th August, which said:

> Dear Father Wain, As you see we are home again in the grime, feeling very thankful for such a marvellous experience, & good weather. Herewith "Timothy", I hope you and your small boys will derive as much help & pleasure from him as we have. ... Did you have a good time with the scouts, or did you miss "Little Audrey"? We had the scouts from Kenton our second week & one evening they attended with us at Benediction in Shrine at the High Altar – it was good!
>
> And Derick Catley's diary has arrived, most interesting. And Bp Nash has sent me a copy of his book, owing to my interest in school chaplainship. I think that's how it will work out in the end. My "talents" point that way – and I am attracted – & I never was potty about parish work (not that anybody ever is!)

For Bishop Nash, see below under St Matthew's Day (September 21st)

Sunday Trinity IX, 1938

> At the 11 o/c Sung Mass after a couple of communicants, about half a dozen others – visitors – made up their minds to "go up" – obviously they didn't know whether they wanted to or not! And 3 of 'em were quite young, probably all one family. I boiled & the vicar boiled & poor Mrs Mackay boiled, & the choir stared, & sang the hymn twice. It served as the occasion, later, for quite a lot of private instruction about fasting

communion, & preparation. Next week, as I'm preaching again, I intend to say a few words & read the BCP 3rd exhortation. It will come better from me than from the Vicar, too – it won't be "one of the Vicar's ideas"!

The Third Exhortation urges intending communicants "diligently to try and examine themselves before they presume to eat of that bread and drink of that cup" warning that "if we receive the same unworthily…we eat and drink our own damnation". It is rarely (never?) used nowadays!

No SS, therefore a bike ride to Haughmond Hill with Geoff Young. [*A local beauty spot, a few miles from Shrewsbury. Nearby is the site of a ruined abbey which was in the care of the Office of Works (now English Heritage).*] Jolly good & awfully hot. He showed me all sorts of things, eg the swallows' nests on the old bridge at Atcham.

Monday. Assumption of Our Lady

We had the proper Mass [*ie. the special one for that day*], & I lent Miss Myott my English Missal.

The Assumption is the belief that the Virgin Mary was taken up into heaven in body as well as in soul. The doctrine was first found in Gnostic circles in the fourth century; 15th August was celebrated as the feast during the Middle Ages. It was not, however, officially defined as an article of faith, even by the Roman Catholic Church, until 1950. For more on this, see below under August 24th.

After Fred Turner's father's funeral (which they wanted

on Sunday, to be quick!) talked to Mr Pugh about undertaking, all the ins & outs. Bertie writes that they were kept waiting for the lorry until 4 o/c – so it's lucky I didn't decide to make use of it [*ie. on 9th August*].

Wednesday 17th August

Today he went to the Shrewsbury Flower Show, first held in the Quarry park in 1875, and still (2006) described as "the longest-running horticultural show in the world to have been held continuously in one location".

Shrewsbury Flower Show – jolly good, but I'm not sure that I'd want to go every year. 7/6 for one thing, but then everything is free inside, & with that ticket one saw the flower tents before the plebs arrived in their thousands. Sandwich lunch there in the Dingle [*colourful sunken gardens at the centre of the show*]. Back for tea, Evensong & supper, & back again for the fireworks (very good), & away just before ten o'clock. The flowers, fruit, veg, bees, etc. were marvellous, & the Grenadier & Coldstream Guards bands magnificent. [*According to the* Shrewsbury Chronicle, *the Band of HM Royal Horse Guards was there also. When the three joined together in the evening, they formed "the largest massed military band ever heard outside London". The Band of the Coldstream Guards is still taking part in the twenty-first century, having now appeared on over sixty occasions.*] Didn't come across Rawlins, tho' I'd arranged to meet him, but met his vicar (Daddy Roach), & Prebendary Salt (who said "they do rook you" [*overcharge*]) & lots of others. Hordes of Popish priests in the morning, & the (K)NOBS! in full force, Lord & Lady Berwick,

Mrs Dugdale, etc etc, Horse leaping, bands, continuous variety, tightrope walking, trapeze people (frightfully good), all ending up with a very high church display of fireworks! & two big balloons. The crowds tomorrow are going to be even vaster (25 buses parked round the Abbey at Evensong). The scenes that old Abbey has witnessed down the centuries! Tomorrow I spend a day in the capacity of verger, showing people round (& keeping an eye on them!)

Lord Berwick was Thomas Henry Noel-Hill, 8th Baron Berwick, who was a retired diplomat and had restored his family seat of Attingham Park, near Shrewsbury. He left his house to the National Trust at his death in 1947. Prebendary William Salt was Rector of Burghfield, Reading, at this time, but up to 1936 had been Rural Dean of Edgmond and Rector of Newport (Shropshire), and Prebendary of Lichfield.

The *Shrewsbury Chronicle*, indulging in the kind of purple passage that newspapers in that period enjoyed, said: "Transformed from a peaceful pleasaunce of rare pastoral and sylvan charm to a veritable fairyland of flowers and music, the Quarry at Shrewsbury witnessed brilliant and thrilling scenes... ." The climax of the "very high church display of fireworks" was the Shrewsbury coat of arms, with the words "*Floreat Salopia*" and "Success to our show", and a portrait of the king.

Monkmoor boys in the S. John Ambulance crowd...

Thursday 18th August

Verging dull in parts, & interesting in parts. In the morning a female Roman convert, who had put a silly note in the clergy box last night. Definitely "queer" (I mean in the head), but pathetically interesting – all about herself. Anyway she knew Bp Frere in her younger days, & he – wisely! – sent her to Farm Street. [*Presumably a reference to the Jesuit Church of the Immaculate Conception in Farm Street, Mayfair.*] Also she designed the original statue of Our Lady of Walsingham [*Added:* LATER: However an article in the Green Quarterly (Autumn 1934) says it was the work of a Carmelite nun. Perhaps it means the actual carving] from the seal in the British Museum. Likes Mr Williams, at Walsingham, but dislikes the Roman spikeshop person, & also the Romans there in general. Anyway, after his experience with her at the old pulpit, our Mr Bilcliffe dislikes <u>her</u> intensely!

According to Colin Stephenson's *Walsingham Way*, the statue was carved by a Carmelite nun, Sister Catherine, at a convent in North Kensington, but Hope Patten "was always slightly mysterious about the origins of the image".

In the afternoon, an old lady from Luton who knows Dennis Bennett, & in the evening a choir outing from Droitwich, & last but not least, a woman feeding a baby in the very pew where I usually meditate! Also after the Roman female, a very knowall boy, who certainly knew all about architecture.

About 8 p.m. my day of vergering drew to a close, as Mr Woodnorth came along to count the takings in the boxes. PC today from Pat Thomas, staying with Fr Dachtler in London, & invitation from Mrs Thos. to go round next week.

Friday 19th August

Tenniquoits and tea at the Lloyd's & then I gave Miss Lloyd's sister a Greek lesson – she shd make v. good progress, has been working already (Nunn's *Elements of N.T. Greek*) and I'm going up regularly every week – & as they <u>insist</u>, I shall earn a useful sum! [*H. P. V. Nunn's* Elements of New Testament Greek *was a school-book originally published in 1914. The fourth edition was published by the Cambridge University Press in 1926.*] Cycling back through the Quarry, got thoroughly drenched, as there was a sudden storm. This morning Roy Blythe sent me a Woggle he made for me in memory of the camp at Kelham.

Those who have never been boy scouts will need to know that a woggle is the ring made of cord, metal or bone, used for tying a scout's scarf or neckerchief! The word is apparently used in the 1929 edition of Baden Powell's *Scouting for Boys*.

I ought to have mentioned that the Roman female yesterday reckoned to have her "feet on the Rock and head in the heavens". She cdn't quite see why I laughed! Anyway she was rather clever, & told me a few things about myself with a queer kind of insight (eg ancestry).

S. Julian's church [*a Saxon church in Shrewsbury High Street, largely rebuilt in 1749-50, now (in 2006) a craft centre*], extremely Prot., evening Communions, etc etc, has been RENOVATED – scrubbed, polished, painted, etc. I had a look in. Rosypink frontal instead of the permanent black one. Now looks less like a cemetery chapel of the bad type, & more like Birmingham Town Hall!

Extract from the magazine: "It seems to be a wish of the majority that we shall have some flowers always placed on the Lord's Table. It can hardly be displeasing to God to decorate His House with His Own beautiful flowers…I will myself set an example by personally providing them for the first Sunday when they will be <u>in use</u> (sic) … Some persons – I do not know why – have associated the presence of flowers in church with unscriptural doctrines. But <u>they will have no doctrinal significance in S. Julian's</u>" (!) It is rather pathetic really because he goes on to refer to his own great age, & prays that his successors will preach nothing but the pure word of God from S. Julian's pulpit. Holt I see is preaching for them during his holiday, as he finds it so difficult to get anyone to help. Well – <u>I</u> wouldn't.

The presence of flowers on the altar was regarded as dangerously high-church in some quarters. Leonard Newby had been ordained priest as far back as 1896, and had been vicar of St Julian's since 1916. For more on him, see the entry for 10th December. The patrons of the living were the Church Patronage Society, an evangelical trust.

Tuesday 23rd August

On Sunday the Thomas's, Pat & Stan, returned from a visit to Fr Dachtler in London, full of instruction! And "Fathering" me like billyo! – incense – Reservation – Lady statues – votive candles – Mass & "Eveningsong"!! I went round there tonight for the evening. Fred & Stan want to be confirmed this time, & both want to make their confessions – but NOT TO THE VICAR! If only he will let Young have them, all will be well – They said Fr Dachtler – but realised the impossibility after a bit. And I do hope I have some to prepare for Confirmation, but it doesn't look like it!

Wednesday 24th August

From today's *Times* "rhinoceros & hippopotamus are bad enough, but can anyone tell us the plural of reredos?"

Here there is a cutting stuck in, a humorous article which discusses the plurals of certain 'difficult' English nouns.

Beastly is the word

A few days ago the SECRETARY of the ZOOLOGI-CAL SOCIETY challenged the word rhinoceri, which appeared in these columns as the plural of rhinoceros. ...Cactus and crocus hardly rank as dilemmata, and abacus is what you would expect. ... But reredos... . Reredos is the limit. Etymology must surely admit defeat. The dictionaries are mum. The cat is off the mat.

... MR. JULIAN HUXLEY...advocates the adoption of rhino and hippo, and pleads tentatively for chimp. The eminent correspondent attacks this expedient, with considerable plausibility, as "leading to a kind of laziness of thinking". There...are...ignorant and idle fellows who, if the "rhino" precedent was adopted, might in correspondence with the Zoo address its secretary as Hux, because they could not remember for certain whether there was an e before the y.

No; abbreviation is an unworthy solution. In the animal world much might be done by employing universally the collective singular. ...The jilted lover who remembers the professional touch in time and announces "I am going out east to shoot tiger" will gain in stature in the eyes of the cruel fair; and the same is probably true of the cruel fair who bids the poor sap go out into the garden and eat worm. But all this is begging the main question. Straining at all these gnat has got us no nearer to swallowing the camel, and reredos is still obstinately singular.

It might seem appropriate to describe this as elephantine humour, but it evidently appealed to FW.

FW's text continues:

After many efforts to "cut down" smoking (which has greatly increased since leaving College), I'm now going to give it up, & save the money in a special box! and buy a Lady statue with it when it has accumulated! [*See below, 31st October.*] Except for big occasions – but they must be big ones – eg holidays.

Mrs Hammond, who had probably never heard of the Assumption in her life before, thought my sermon on Sunday was <u>lovely</u>. It was this dear old soul who said of the incense (when she met it for the first time): "I can't understand what they make a fuss about – I think it's a <u>lovely</u> smell!"

Saturday 27th August

This morning Mr Bilcliffe rang the bell for Mass at 7.30 instead of 8 (forgetting it was Saturday!) Out of bed I shot! But I was the only one he disturbed, as the vicarage is too far to hear. His daughter had let him go out without saying a word! Mrs Lloyd & I held a consultation as to what day it was…after all, I ought to have been up in any case by then! Memories of George Walker ringing the rising bell at HOR [*Hostel of the Resurrection*] at 5.30 a.m., & Bags scuttling round, already up! I've been thinking about Mirfield quite a lot the last few days.

Friday 2nd September

Quite cold the last 2 or 3 days, & the suspicion of a frost in the mornings – & now quite dark as I bike back from Miss L's Greek class. The curfew ringing at S. Mary's. One way traffic now, too, in the town. Tonight to the Thomas's again – to peel onions for pickling! But we didn't do many – Pat was too busy reading *She* which I had lent them [*the adventure story by H Rider Haggard, which more than twenty years later he recommended to his eight-year old son as "the most spooky story I ever read"*], & Stan & Fred found the whole business too weepy, while Mrs Thomas had a lot of unexpected sewing & Sheila came home too late. My eyes stood it well, & I did a jar-full.

Saturday 3rd September

This morning my books arrived from the S.P.C.K. – Deacon's grant, & I spent a lot of time that shd have been otherwise used in arranging them. They make a most imposing array – the book on the Carthusian Martyrs, & Neale, & the "King's Book", & a lot of biographies. Fr Symonds' new book is coming too, as soon as published. [*This will have referred to* The Church Universal and the See of Rome, *which was published by the SPCK for the Church Historical Society in 1939. FW had a copy with* January 1939 *on the fly-leaf.*] A great surprise when I came in from the magazine round – a letter from Audrey! She'd asked Fr Taylor if "Shrewsbury Abbey" wd find me – so she evidently means it – hooray!

Amongst his surviving books in 2002 was Conrad Noel's *The Life of Jesus*, London, Dent, 1937, with the fly-leaf dated October 1938. If the date was that of reading rather than of purchase, it is not unlikely that that was amongst the books here referred to. A slightly surprising choice, as FW's politics were never those of Conrad Noel (Christian Socialist) – though their respective theological views were much more in accord!

The "King's Book" referred to above is presumably the book of doctrine produced with the royal authority in 1543, marking a stage in the development of Henry VIII's "Catholicism without the pope". The sub-title was "A necessary doctrine and erudition for any Christian man". There was a modern edition by T A Lacey, published by the SPCK for the Church Historical Society in 1932.

Sunday Trinity XI

SS started again – a very sober class & a good lesson, & 4 <u>intelligent</u> new boys! Then for a walk thro' the Dun Cow [*a pub in Abbey Foregate not far from FW's digs*] & down by the brook with Geoff Young & Jim Braddock. Sad event: Tony Lovell's voice is breaking – it was the loveliest boy's voice I've heard – a treat to be near him in the stalls at Mass – "Hosanna (pom) hosanna (pom) hosanna-in-the-highest…!"And he always put all he knew into it – sounds like an obituary notice, but quite the contrary, he's only growing up!

Monday 5th September

This afternoon arrived, from Miss Daniel, a few prints of me at Walsingham, which will be useful, and also – a copy of the magazine of Audrey's parish – Kenton. It's (as one expected) an absolutely magnificent catholic place.

Mary Daniel's letter quoted above (13th August) said: "We have only just had the films developed, they are rather disappointing, but I'll send some prints that I think you will find interesting later." FW's photograph album for the relevant period includes a number of snaps of boys on the scouting holiday, but nothing obviously relating to Walsingham.

Wednesday 7th September

Yesterday – measurements for Miss Y [i.e. Missionary] Exhibition. Today: wrote to Audrey. Tonight – a supper party at Miss Ormiston's. All the men invited couldn't come, except me, so it was somewhat quaint!

More will be heard of the Missionary exhibition and its associated play later. The *Shrewsbury Chronicle* for 30th September carried a notice, phrased in a more patronising tone than would be used today:

Visit "Africa" in Shrewsbury! Impossible, you will say. Then visit the Music Hall, Shrewsbury, during the week October 6-12 and see for yourselves. See the African church with its native priest, the African school with its native teacher and class, and note their willingness to learn. You may also inspect the hospital, the goal of poor natives suffering from disease or injury by animals which prowl around the outskirts of the village. Compare conditions of living in your own land with those of the African in his hut, and count your blessings. Meanwhile, learn, too, what missionaries are doing for these people to improve their lot in life, to help them to know the true God, and hear what part you may play in this important branch of the church's work. You cannot fail to be moved by what you will see and hear. Come to "Africa" – do not miss this opportunity – and bring your friends.

Thursday 8th September – Nativ. B.V.M.

The Choir Outing to New Brighton, via Birkenhead & Liverpool. 24 boys, but not many men – Mr Turner, Messrs Woodnorth, Bilcliffe, Halford, Cecil Gibbs, Cecil Love, Arthur Russell & Mr Chapman. Mrs L got me a good breakfast early, & at half past 7 I dashed out & joined Jimmie Hughes who was running & intending to run the whole way! But I firmly dissuaded him.

They were awfully thrilled by the Museum at Liverpool, skeletons, animals, birds, ships, aquarium – <u>mummies</u>. Strange that most of them didn't know about mummies!

The museum, a monument to Victorian civic pride, was built to house the 13th Earl of Derby's natural history collection, which he bequeathed to the town in 1851. In 2006 it is still a good museum, though naturally set out in a more up-to-date style – and the mummies are still there!

A very good lunch at the *Stork*. Jim Braddock was looking for a conduit in Liverpool, but we couldn't even find a water fountain. On the way to the ferry there was an "oo Look!" as we passed Tucker's church shop – the windows full of every variety of ecclesiastical ornament. Eventually bought 3 crucifixes for those who lingered with me – most were afraid of getting left behind. These were Alwyn, Jim Braddock, & Gordon Backhouse. They'd been given a bob to get their own tea, but some spent the last ha'penny before then in the fair ground. The "Figure of 8" jolly good, & we saw Al Capone's car for 2d.

Then Alwyn, Alan Young & Kenny Parker & I had a proper tea in a café, which they enjoyed. Otherwise they'd have had a pennorth of chips & a bottle of pop like Ralph Stones, I expect. I took these three on the big boating pool after tea (Alan better than Alwyn when they attempted to row), & we were then just in time to catch the 6.15 ferry back. I was in charge of 12 of the smaller fry, since the main party didn't arrive home till 1.30 a.m. We deposited Alan Rickard with his parents at Liverpool, & arrived home without any untoward incident at 9.30 (except that George Davies "didn't feel very well" and cried hard, but that was due to some of 'em smoking in the other compartment!). On the English Bridge we met old Miss Bennett who keeps the 2nd hand bookshop, & she said to them "You must love your minister, don't you?"

Then Jimmie Hughes revealed the fact that there wd be no one in at his house, & he wd only have a drink of water before going to bed, so we bought 4 pennyworths of chips in the Foregate & ate them in my digs with a *Times* spread out across the table. Mrs Lloyd supplied cups of cocoa, & it was very nice. This was Alwyn, Jimmie & Donald Davies. When I told Alwyn to hang his crucifix by his bed so he cd see it when he said his prayers, he said "But I always shut my eyes when I say my prayers!" Jimmie said he kneeled <u>on</u> the bed to say his, so if he had one he would hang it <u>over</u> the bed!

An album full of the world's most sentimental "First mass" cards has arrived from B.O.W., but it looks as if I shall have to make my choice from them.

A copy of the one he used in fact survives, a bookmark in his well-used copy of *The Priest's Book of Private Devotion*. Sentimental? Well, perhaps. (See entry for October 2nd.)

Friday 9th September

A long drive with Mr & Miss & Mrs Dovey to the Horseshoe Pass & back this evening, followed by supper at Prestfelde. Begin to realise how I've depended on Prestfelde, & how I've been missing it.

Horseshoe Pass is near Llangollen – perhaps forty miles from Shrewsbury, certainly a long drive on the roads of 1938! Mr Dovey was the headmaster of Prestfelde, as mentioned above on 18th July.

Sunday, Trinity XIII 1938

The boys sang Harwood magnificently this morning. Young has returned, & read my *Si Quis*, & was horrified to hear about Audrey! Some more new boys @ SS & from the Priory too! [*the school in Shrewsbury*] Now I want to "go up" with them next year instead of having a new lot of small ones. Tonight's wireless – if Hitler attacks Czechoslovakia, France will go to their aid (& is ready), & if France needs it, we shall help, & then America. I should imagine it's all to make Hitler see he's got everybody against him – but he may not! It's awfully serious & will be a narrow escape if it succeeds – Runciman at Prague, etc.

Viscount Runciman, the Lord President of the Council, the former National Liberal MP, had been sent to Prague to act as a mediator in July. Negotiations had been going on through the summer but no one took the Western powers' promises of support to Czechoslovakia very seriously. On 4th September, Beneš, the president of Czechoslovakia, agreed to all the demands of the Sudeten Germans, but by then he knew that this would not satisfy them.

Monday 12th September

A visit from Mr & Mrs Hart today, on their way north – 3.20 to 5.20, & they saw S. Mary's & the Abbey (vastly preferring the Abbey) & had a quick tea. Mr H. very thrilled indeed with the Abbey, but shocked at the way we keep the tombs – I cd have told him a lot more shocking things, but only mentioned the Altar Linen. …

Tuesday 13th September

1st Rehearsal for the Missionary play – quite a good attendance, but we are short of men & I shall have to make it up with boys. Fr Hambling came & it went off quite well – but oh Mrs W!

Wednesday – *HOLY CROSS DAY 1938*

Masses at 7.30 & 9.30 – we should have a much larger attendance daily, I'm sure, if only it was at 7 o/c. About 20 <u>in all</u>. I served Young at 9.30. Much rushing round, getting a plain Yes or No out of people, drawing up the CAST (finally) for *Africa* [*the missionary play referred to above*].

If ever the outlook was black, it is today. They have published an ultimatum about not being responsible for the consequences in Germany.

On 13th there was a revolt by the Sudeten Germans which the Czech government crushed. The French government sent an urgent message to Neville Chamberlain saying that the entry of German troops into Czechoslovakia must be avoided at all costs, which gave him a free hand to redress German grievances in order to prevent this.

Thursday 15th September

This morning the Prime Minister, Mr Chamberlain, flew to Germany to try and bring about a peaceful settlement between Hitler & Czechoslovakia. [*He flew to Munich and saw Hitler at Berchtesgaden.*] Peter

Conduit's father is a military man, & when I went round to see if Peter cd be Boat Boy in the play, he was quite expecting to be called up soon. This morning Peter had a fit of shyness & doesn't want to be in it after all (he is so very little) so we've had to have Cyril Cox instead.

Preparations were still going on for the Missionary Exhibition and Play, which eventually took place in October, the exhibition opening on 6th, the play being performed on 10th.

Tonight an Executive meeting – probably the last – at which all the skeletons in the cupboards came out. We went on quite late, & Fr Hambling lost his temper, & the Rural Dean's sense of humour deserted him at last, & Fr Mackenzie sat & sulked the whole time. Whoopee! When I told Fr M our vicar didn't think it at all necessary for me to rehearse the Mass – he replied "HE WOULDN'T!" I met their Miss Alston in town this morning, & she was sarcastic (as indeed everybody is) about the blessed Exhibition. We seem to have our part much better in hand than they have, & many of the other courts have done just nothing about it! Especially S. Alkmund's – where the Vicar is leaving for Bermuda, & Holt, when he returns from his holidays, will depart immediately to be priested!

"Courts" appears to refer to the individual areas where the tableaux were to be presented, each in the charge of a different one of the Shrewsbury churches.

Had to refuse an invitation to "talk about turnips" to the people of Oxon [*on the outskirts of Shrewsbury*], but I'm going later to Pitchford – my first Harvest festival for 7 yrs!

Cutting pasted in from *The Times* of 15th September:

> NEVILLE CHAMBERLAIN
> As Priam to Achilles for his Son,
> So you, into the night, divinely led,
> To ask that young men's bodies, not yet dead,
> Be given from the battle not begun.
> JOHN MASEFIELD

Masefield was poet laureate. Best remembered now for a few poems about the sea, he was a veteran of the Gallipoli campaign – about which he wrote in similarly bombastic terms – and had worked for the War Propaganda Bureau. The reference is to the *Iliad,* Book XXIV, in which Priam pleads with Achilles for the body of the dead Hector. Chamberlain, in contrast, was pleading with Hitler before the young men were slain.

Friday 16th September

Addressing ordination cards – coffee with Rawlins at Morris's – Judith Butts visits – tea at Prestefelde (Preb. & Mrs Norcock & Michael also there) – rushing round the shops with *Africa* Posters – & SS Association meeting. They <u>almost</u> voted not to have refreshments at this year's meetings, but Rawlins & I stopped 'em!

Judith Butts refers to a street of council houses within the parish of the Abbey. The name Butts is either from archery or perhaps refers to land abutting onto a boundary.

Shrewsbury Carnival was yesterday – quite good, but I saw only the procession (with the S. Saviour's children at the bottom of Wyle Cop [*one of the principal roads in the central part of Shrewsbury. The name means 'Hill top' in Welsh.*]) The beauty Queens, from all over the neighbourhood, were awful hags – Shropshire would appear to be an exceedingly ill-favoured spot!

A very hasty and later-revised opinion, I am sure! The *Shrewsbury Chronicle* described Miss Shropshire as "this lovely fair-haired girl with the luminous grey-blue eyes, ... passionately fond of dancing and loves tennis and swimming". She had been chosen by the comedy actress Jeanne de Casalis, the star of early broadcasting and the creator of "Mrs Feather". She was attended by "sixty-five lovely girls who have been chosen at dances arranged for the purpose in towns and villages of Shropshire," and their photographs are recorded for posterity in the *Shrewsbury Chronicle*!

Little Johnny Creame solemnly sent me his love *per* Audrey the other day.

We may think Audrey's letter the real reason for FW's grudging attitude to the beauty queens!

Other events in the carnival, which raised £1530 for the Shrewsbury hospitals, included a boxing tournament, a Flitch trial, a baby show, a Ladies' football match and a half-mile swimming race down the Severn.

Sunday within Octave of Holy Cross, 1938

[*The formal name of the Abbey is the Parish Church of the Holy Cross, so this was the patronal festival.*] About 90 communicants – including most of the young ones (Fred T – who is going to the R.A.F. at the end of the month, Colin & Mostyn). A good crowd at 11 for HM & Procn [High Mass and Procession] – very happy, but more tiring than usual, owing to the absence of Tom Brown, who was practically MC. [*Master of Ceremonies.*] The Vicar alas, preached for nearly 20 mins – the poor children!

To Prestefelde after SS for a 1st Mass rehearsal with Young, & tea. This made me late for Solemn Evensong – at which I presided – so I was continually worrying whether I'd got the right books. All was very nice, & the servers turned east obediently at all the proper times, & even bowed & made the sign of the Cross. Another futile sermon. But my word, how they sang *Lift High the Cross!* (likewise this morning), and then the Te Deum (Martin) went absolutely magnificently – it was a great joy, & all the people in church whom one wanted. I had to make dear Colin spit out his chewing gum before we left the Vestry! It's scarcely believable, but then, they've hardly had any training at all. Afterwards Tony & Ray Davies & one or two others wanted to know about Audrey – when would the wedding be? Could they come? My hat!! After SS, Ralph Stones said "I was a good boy this afternoon, wasn't I?" And when I was speaking about prayers, at SS, and said how when we've finished those we know by heart, we shd try just "talking to God" – Bobby Davies turned round

1 Frank Wain as a curate. The photograph was taken in 1939.

2 Shrewsbury Abbey, as it was before the war.

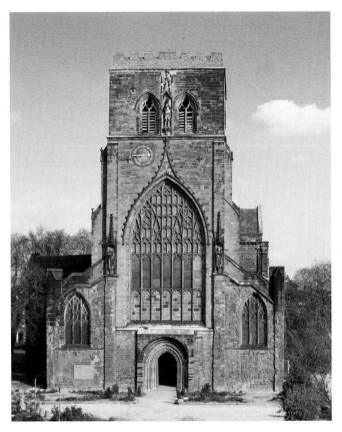

3 The west front of Shrewsbury Abbey.

4 The Chapel of the Resurrection, Mirfield. Here stood the baldaccino from which the cat appeared during Compline. (Thursday 7th July)

5 *The church at Mirfield as described on the day of its dedication,*
Wednesday 6th July.

6 *The Quarry Theatre, where* St Joan *was performed*
later the same day.

7 Lichfield Cathedral from the north-west. Canon Hammond's house, where Frank was wakened by the bell for Prime at 6 a.m. on Tuesday 12th July, would have been down the hill to the photographer's right.

8 South Creake. "England's most beautiful church". (Thursday 28th July)

9 Walsingham, the interior of the Holy House, traditionally of the same dimensions as that at Nazareth.

10 The ruins of Walsingham Abbey, which gave an opportunity to tell the cubs about Henry VIII. (Sunday 31st July)

11 The sepulchre in the garden at Walsingham, which the cubs weren't allowed into. (Sunday 31st July)

12 *Walsingham, the exterior of the shrine. This photograph was taken in 1931, the year it was opened.*

13 *Southwell Minster, where Frank went up the tower, but his companions "didn't enjoy the heights!" (Thursday 4th August)*

14 The Bishop's Palace, at Lichfield. "Well sir, we 'aven't quite decided w'ere to put you yet, sir." (Thursday 29th September)

15 (left) The choir of Lichfield Cathedral, showing the Bishop's throne.

16 (below) The ordinands were "led by the Archdeacon and presented in the Sanctuary". (Sunday 2nd October)

17 The crossing, with the pulpit. Canon B K Cunningham said he'd never preached on such an "elevated perch". (Sunday 2nd October)

18 One of "the interesting things I love" which Frank showed the boys (Sunday 2nd October) will have been The Sleeping Children, *Sir Francis Chantrey's famous monument to Ellen-Jane and Marianne, the tragic daughters of Prebendary William Robinson.*

& said to somebody – in <u>such</u> a Shropshire accent – "Do <u>you</u> do that? <u>I</u> do!" It was beautiful.

Monday 19th September

To Mirfield [*for a Retreat*] by the 7.28 a.m. Got out of the train at 7.30 just in time to avoid being carried off to Ludlow, Salop! There had been two close together, & mine had gone without me. So to Mass at S. Mary's (8 o/c), said, I think, by a prospective curate. Then by the 9.10 to Mirfield. By catching a Leeds express at Stalybridge, & a bus from Huddersfield, I got in half an hour earlier, just in time for lunch at 1.15. We passed through a lot of thick fog around Stockport.

It was, as usual, a great joy to be back, the place & the people. "Peace seems to rest upon it". Ron Lewis [*a college contemporary, then Curate of St Cuthbert's, Brislington, Bristol, with whom FW stayed in touch till Ron's death in 2000*] walked in about 3 o/c while I was talking to Reg Gurnham in his room (Retreat House). Both of them are very full of the subject of girls – or dames, as <u>they</u> call it – but I don't! Both perfectly happy in their parishes. Meals in the House Refec very jolly, waited on by the Brethren. Mr Rose is here, but has his with the older ones, in a separate room during the time of the Retreat. He calls them the old Boys, and doesn't enjoy it very much. Bill & I talked to him in his room after supper.

At Evensong of course the College were present, & there were all those whom we used to call Hostel Boys – and old Shuffle was among them! But there were several gaps, and since there were at least half a dozen failures in GOE [*General Ordination Exam*] (Nobby, Bennion, Burt [*Added:* ?], Paton, Crawshaw, Southcott, at least) the Orate list is short. [*All these named, apart from the unidentifiable Nobby, were ordained in 1938 – so they are evidently ones who had passed their exams and were on the Orate list to be prayed for.*] And I hear that Tom [*Hannay*] is tightening things up – padlocks on the old Kitchen door & the underground – & no black-sheets – they are numbered off at Mattins instead. Time too – we were getting very lax. Well, the singing at Evensong was unaccompanied since the Hammond organ was only temporary, but it wasn't so bad. Compline was really lovely. A gorgeous hot bath, & to bed.

Tuesday 20th September (vigil of S. Matthew)

Up at 6.15, Mattins 6.50. Prime & Mass. Spare breakfast, being the vigil! The Retreat addresses are good, but ordinary, well, it's not possible to barge in in the middle of a Retreat & do it properly (a little talking to Ron). Nevertheless it is a genuine time of refreshment & prayer. It's impossible to come to Mirfield and find it otherwise! Fr <u>Evans,</u> I find, is the Retreat Conductor (in Africa all the while I was at College). Very stern about giving ourselves to God. He said most Christians are like a gardener planting artificial flowers in a garden, & sprinkling a little perfume over them to deceive the bees. John Graham, it turns out afterwards, thought he said "beans"! The echo made it hard to hear him, but one quickly got used to it. In the Upper Church it is a Resonance, rather than an echo, & one of the delightful results is the pause at the colon in the Psalms is much longer, as they wait for it to die away. I love it.

Fr William Evans had been Curate of St Paul's, Rondebosch, from 1935 to 1938.

Solemn Evensong tonight very lovely & dignified – the procession really beautiful, & well spaced. Tonight & last night awake for ages – it has only just dawned on me that the reason is the coffee at supper – though it is as early as half past 7. Now I have Freud's most interesting book *The Significance of Dreams* from the House Library – so I have plenty to occupy me! [*It seems an odd book to be reading on retreat!*] At supper at the House one of the novices has only bread & milk (properly, not like Fr Gerard) – & another has a glass of stout – both lay novices. Ron Lewis is nearly 14 stone, & urges me to take up Ovaltine every night as he does – & I urge him to give it up – he really doesn't need to get any heavier!

S. MATTHEW'S DAY

In time for Mattins (Athanasian Creed) & Prime & Mass – High Mass, most beautiful & dignified, really a great joy.

The Athanasian Creed is the third of the historic creeds of the Church; it may be found in the Book of Common Prayer after Evensong, and the rubric orders it to be used on thirteen major festivals, including St Matthew's Day. This is another piece of the rite which has been heard in use by scarcely any present-day Anglicans. It consists primarily of a series of very narrowly drawn definitions of the doctrines of the Trinity and the Incarnation, together with dreadful anathemas pronounced on those who do not accept them.

> Another procession – actually I'm quite glad they are cutting down the number of processions: Eves of Saints' Days, every Sunday, Litany in procession, & high festivals, a procession before Mass. But the regular Saturday Evening, & Saints' Day mornings are to be cut out.

> Mr Rose left early at the end of Mass. Fr Viccy was Clerk, as they've not yet got the ceremonies straightened for the new Sanctuary. Silence of Retreat broken, & breakfast at the College – sat with R.J. Visited all the staff – I mean domestic – long chat with Fr V.S. in his room after tea, and another with Bp Nash after supper.

VS was Victor Shearburn, a member of the CR who was later an army chaplain in Burma and subsequently Bishop of Rangoon. James Nash was the last surviving Founder member of the Community. Before retirement he had been co-adjutor Bishop of Cape Town, and before that Headmaster of St John's College, Johannesburg.

> Then my confession (Fr V.S.), near S Mary Magdalene's altar in the Upper Church – very stern about meditation! I've got to start again promptly! The Blessed Sacrament being now at the Resurrection Altar – as lovely as ever at night – and the new position of the Lady Statue – all very nice. There were some photos

of the statue, but I only got two, as they'd sold out –
one for Audrey & one for the Vicar. A last chat with
Ron after Compline – & then to sleep easily. There
is a Russian at the College, with long hair.

Thursday 22nd September

By the 10.21 to Battyford – with one of the stranger-
priests who had been at the Retreat (from Cardiff).
And the train didn't stop at Stalybridge so to Manchester & across the city to the other station, Crewe
at 1 o/c & Shrewsbury at 1.56 – dead on time! Met
Tony Lovell & his sister in the Foregate – how he
grinned! Masses of letters waiting for me, among them
one from Kenneth Steege's mother; he passed away
on August 5th. Why did nobody mention it at Mirfield?
Of course Frs Hannay & VS wouldn't be likely to tell
everybody, & the prayer notices wd be taken down &
I've not heard from Cecil Sayer for some time. His
mother sends a small photo. He had a chill, followed
by pneumonia – of course he would be unable to stand
anything like that. He was expecting to be ordained
Deacon this week.

A letter from an old college friend, George Burningham,
dated 6th June 1989, says "I keep Steege's year's mind on Aug.
5th, the same as Perkins 50 years later. I remember cycling
out from Guildford along the Pillingbourne Valley to visit
Steege in his sanatorium at Witley shortly before his death."

The international situation has eased a great deal –
probably Hitler will have the parts of Czechoslovakia
he wants – but all manner of surrounding nations want

to share in the carving up of the unhappy country! Rehearsal for the Missionary playlet, in the Lady Chapel – went well, most people there.

K.S. was very good to me when I was a mere fresher at Leeds, & I have always been grateful. He was always the same, whenever we met, always so <u>sane,</u> and able to help a bloke like me. Even to talk to him – even if only to grumble to him. Though I know he worried himself about all sorts of things, it never affected this. Now he is in his Father's hands, where there is nothing to worry about, & we know all is well with him. Such a friend as one can really thank God for. I think that will always be my feeling. And how he suffered in his long illness we can never know.

Thomas Hannay in *The Mirfield Gazette*, Martinmas 1938, p.32, indicates that Steege had been repeatedly ill with tuberculosis and appendicitis since his arrival at the college as early as 1929. The only child of his parents, "quiet, reserved, with an armour not easily penetrated, he yet was well liked, and played a real part in College life".

Friday 23rd September

Said Evensong for them at S Mary's – then to the flicks – Ian Hay's *Housemaster* & very good. [*A film set in a public school, based on a 1936 novel by Hay and starring Otto Kruger.*] Also a <u>good</u> Laurel & Hardy. There was an A.R.P. appeal on the screen too, local. In spite of the alleviation, the situation has become tense again, & Mr Chamberlain had to return from his latest visit without seeing Hitler at all!

On 15th September Chamberlain at Berchtesgaden had offered Hitler the complete separation of the Sudeten Germans from the rest of Czechoslovakia. On 18th, Daladier, the French premier, asked him whether he would guarantee the new, smaller Czechoslovakia, which Chamberlain, without consulting the cabinet apart from three colleagues, Halifax, Simon and Hoare, agreed to do. On 22nd, Chamberlain went back to Germany, met Hitler at Godesberg on the Rhine, and found that Hitler had raised his demands from the transfer of territory after negotiation to immediate occupation. As FW said on 22nd, the Poles and Hungarians were also making claims on Czechoslovak territory. Hitler had finally agreed not to act before 1st October.

A few days later the *Shrewsbury Chronicle* carried notices:

It is considered probable that if war should occur rationing of foodstuffs would be introduced at an early date.... . In the meantime, the public are advised not to get alarmed about food supplies or to form food queues at shops. Until food control is introduced, retailers should issue to the customers no more of any food commodity than is usually supplied. There is no justification for consumers buying more than their usual requirements...

The distribution of gas masks is in progress and first aid posts and shelters are being put into commission, but it should be emphasised that the emergency for which these preparations are being made has not yet arisen.

It also carried articles on *How to use the gas mask* and *How to dig a shelter trench*, illustrated by appropriate photographs.

Saturday 24th September

> Coffee @ Morris's with Rawlins, where we saw Arthur Russell. … Embertide intercession at S Mary's, conducted by Fr M. He read to us from the *Imitation*, & we also prayed about the international situation – he was very good, but it all looks blacker than ever. "The Lord is King, be the people never so impatient."

The Ember days are four groups of days each year, shortly after which ordinations take place – as FW's on this occasion. The *Imitation of Christ* is a famous late mediaeval devotional manual, usually attributed to St Thomas à Kempis. The quotation is from the opening of Psalm 99.

Sunday 25th September: Trinity XV

> Preached at P.H. – no pianist turned up, lectern broken, lights bad. We said the psalms, & sang 3 hymns unaccompanied – anyway we had full Evensong for a change, & didn't do at all badly. The congregation smaller, but the collection larger than usual! Met Lily Love afterwards – she & Leonard & Victor had been on the Stretton Hills & the chain of the motorbike broke. Then to the Thomas's @ Meole [*in the suburbs of Shrewsbury*] (Vicar & Mrs W having gone to Walsall for S Luke's Harvest Festival). Fred going to R.A.F. for "attestation" on Thursday. This afternoon I went

in to the P.H. (SS) to tell the little ones about AFRICA
– highly successful! Fr Hambling (preaching @ Abbey)
knew Cedric F., & Timms & Breed. ...

Cedric Frank, George Timms and Kenneth Breed had both
been two years ahead of FW at the College, and had served
curacies in Coventry; the first was still there. FW and Breed
were to meet again twenty-three years later when their
respective sons were both entrance candidates at the cathedral
school at Lichfield.

Monday 26th September

Arranged with Tom Brown (at Meole) to bring a few
boys to the ordination – they are all awfully pleased.
Rehearsal for Africa rather tiring – but I speeded up
the plainsong hymn (*contra* Vicar & Mrs W!). Round
to Lowell's to arrange for Sunday with Tony – saw him
& Jean, & Jean's boyfriend – a policeman! And I got
some snaps of Tony! The wireless says they will come
round issuing gas masks to all & sundry quite soon.

Thirty-eight million gas masks were distributed to regional
centres. At the same time trenches were dug in the London
parks, and the total supply of anti-aircraft guns (forty-four)
was made operational. A scheme for the evacuation of
schoolchildren from London was hastily prepared, and eighty-
three per cent of parents applied for their children to go.

Tuesday 27th September

Told the Anson class boys about the Bad period in the
18th C. [*Together with Henry VIII and the Puritan period,*

this was another of FW's bêtes noires *in church history!*]
This afternoon one of the most longwinded R.D. [*Rural
Decanal*] Chapters it wd be possible to imagine! And
when Daddy Roach had finished talking about the
study circle with the Free Church Ministers, Agnew
of S. George's announced that there is already one in
existence in the town! So we didn't have to vote after
all. On arriving home – found that the men had been
round with gasmasks – we all have one, & Tiger is
going to have a bag – bet he won't go into it! Everybody
seems to imagine the Germans will make a beeline for
Shrewsbury instead of Czechoslovakia! Howard Green
writes to say he has a Roman Catholic one!! [*Sic –
presumably a Roman Catholic gasmask.*]

This morning's Psalms: I labour for peace, but when I
speak to them thereof, they make them ready to battle.
And tonight: My peace – not as the world giveth, give
I unto you. [*The first text is Psalm 120, v. 6, the first
psalm appointed for the 27th morning of the month. The
other is from John 14, v. 27, which* An alternative table
of lessons *(1922, revised 1928) does indeed appoint for
Evensong on the Tuesday after the fifteenth Sunday after
Trinity.*] Mr Chamberlain made a speech by wireless
to the whole Empire this evening at 8 o/c – I heard it
across the road at Woodnorth's, & he was very, very good.

That day Chamberlain had ordered the fleet to be
mobilised. Public opinion, a few days before indignant at the
bullying of a small state, had turned to a mood of apprehension.
The speech referred to is reported in the following day's *Times*,
a cutting from which FW pasted into his diary. He was clearly
very conscious of the historic significance of the occasion.

Wednesday 28th September

[*Cutting labelled:*] MR CHAMBERLAIN'S SPEECH. THE TIMES, 28.9.38.

TO THE NATION AND EMPIRE

"IF WE HAVE TO FIGHT"

The Prime Minister broadcast to the nation and the Empire last night a message in which he spoke of his efforts to promote a peaceful solution of the crisis and declared his resolve to work until the last moment for peace.

Chamberlain said that it had been heart-breaking to read the letters he had received from "mothers or sisters of our own countrymen" and also from "countless others in France and Belgium and Italy, and even from Germany", showing their " growing anxiety…and their intense relief when they thought, too soon, that the danger of war was passed".

Such letters have made my responsibility seem almost overwhelming. How horrible, fantastic, and incredible it is that we should be digging trenches and trying on gas masks here because of a quarrel in a far away country between people of whom we know nothing. It seems still more impossible that a quarrel which has already been settled in principle should be the subject of war.

IF TIME WERE ALLOWED

...I have done all that one man can do to compose this quarrel. ... I realize vividly how Herr Hitler feels that he must champion brother Germans. ... He told me privately, and last night he repeated publicly, that after this Sudeten German question is settled, that is the end of Germany's territorial claims in Europe.

After my first visit to Berchtesgaden I did get the assent of the Czech Government to proposals which gave the substance of what Herr Hitler offered. I was taken completely by surprise when I got back to Germany and found that Herr Hitler insisted that the territory should be handed over to him immediately...without previous arrangements for safeguarding the people within the territory who were not Germans. ...

UNREASONABLE

...I shall not give up hope of a peaceful solution, or abandon my efforts for peace, so long as any chance ...remains...

Meanwhile there are certain things we can and should do at home. Volunteers are still wanted for air raid precautions, for fire brigade and police services, and Territorial units. ...

Do not be alarmed if you hear of men being called up to man the anti-aircraft defences or ships. These are only precautionary measures such as a Government must take in times like this. But they do not necessarily mean we have determined on war or that war is imminent.

"IF WE HAVE TO FIGHT"

...For the present I ask you to await as calmly as you can the events of the next few days. ...There is always hope that [war] may be prevented, and you know I am going to work for peace to the last moment. Goodnight.

Another cutting gives the chronology of the crisis, starting the previous March. A third cutting is the leading article:

THE ISSUE DEFINED

...The two Houses of Parliament reassemble this afternoon [to] confront a situation that...moves at last to an issue as simple as it is momentous. For the opportunity to take great decisions in a clear light they have to thank above all the PRIME MINISTER.

...The future political allegiance of the homogeneous German population in Czechoslovakia is no longer in dispute: with the acquiescence of their present rulers and the consent of every Government in Europe they are to be united to their kinsfolk under the flag of the Reich.... Self-determination, the professed principle of the Treaty of Versailles, has been invoked by HERR HITLER against its written text, and his appeal has been allowed. What remains is no more than a question of procedure... . But...the choice is now between the method of reason and the method of force. Czechoslovakia, persuaded by Great Britain and France, has agreed to let the Sudeten Germans go. ...PRESIDENT BENESH and his Government tacitly assumed that all these delicate matters would be adjusted by the civilized method of negotiation. HERR HITLER proposes...to settle them by sending his army to seize the territory that he has already been promised shall not be withheld...

...The hope of peace turns on the possibility of discerning reason where on the surface are only threats, and of appealing...persuasively to this rational element... . Two such appeals of the highest significance have been made in the last thirty-six hours. ...PRESIDENT ROOSEVELT...called upon Prague and Berlin impartially to pause on the brink of irremediable catastrophe; [and] MR CHAMBERLAIN, making yet one more courageous stand for peace, pledged the credit of Great Britain as an alternative to German force to secure the Sudeten Germans against the danger that HERR HITLER professed to see. It...is one of the most tragic features of the perilous situation, that neither of these appeals has been published in Germany. The German people...are...possessed by a genuine longing for peace, and in particular for friendship with England; it is a grievous reflection that they are prevented from knowing that such peace and friendship are offered to them on honourable terms. The...people of a totalitarian State can be approached only through its head, and the basis of conciliation can be sought only in the utterances of HERR HITLER himself... . [*This last ellipsis was added by FW.*]

The editorial writer summed up the facts accurately enough, though with retrospect we may be doubtful whether his optimistic conclusion could reasonably be deduced from them.

Wednesday 28th September (Eve of S. Michael)

About tea time there was a wireless announcement of which I only heard the end – something about Parliament getting up to its feet & cheering. It turns out later that Hitler has promised not to mobilise for another 24 hours (the ultimatum was for 2 pm today, for some reason brought forward from Saturday). The Czechs won't give way, & indeed can't be expected to… . But Hitler has invited Chamberlain, Deladier and Mussolini to go & talk it over in MUNICH [*altered from* Berlin(?)] immediately. Quite likely he wants to climb down – he wd certainly be mad to carry on with nearly everybody against him. [*Added at foot of page:* P.S. The suggestion came from Mussolini.]

This was the occasion on which Chamberlain's speech was dramatically interrupted by a message passed from Halifax, on the peers' gallery, via Dunglass (the future prime minister, Alec Douglas Home), Hoare and Simon, carrying the news of Hitler's acceptance of a four-power conference at Munich. "MPs rose to their feet, cheering and sobbing", in the words of A J P Taylor. Harold Nicolson and the Communist Willie Gallagher were amongst the few who remained seated; as to whether Churchill, Eden and Amery did so, there is some disagreement amongst historians.

Queen Mary, who was watching from the Gallery of the House of Commons, recorded in her diary: "It was a most dramatic and wonderful ending to the speech, and the relief felt all round the House was remarkable and all the members of the Conservative and National Govt cheered wildly – I was so much moved I could not speak. ... A most wonderful day – God be praised."

Anyway, our Social fixed for tonight is cancelled, since the hall has been commandeered & is full of gasmasks. We are also having an executive meeting to decide whether to abandon the Miss'y Exhibition. I want to carry on – The Kingdom of God...etc...but we must admit that if hostilities broke out, the people wouldn't come – & they might want to bag the Music hall. As it is, the meeting is in our West Vestry, since S. Mary's hall is full of gasmasks!

Later – the choir were singing magnificently the whole time (at practice). Only a small gathering – Fr Hambling, Young, Renfree, Mrs W & the Vicar, Miss O, Muriel, Mr Taylor, & Canon Headlam – we discovered, after reckoning everything up, that we should lose more financially if we cancelled it now, than if we carry on & are obliged to do so by the Govt, or thro' loss of the Hall. The stuff from London has got to set out immediately, or it won't get here, as transport has been commandeered. Fr Hambling had come straight from London, & says 1914 was nothing in comparison! The railway stations, etc. Telephones blocked, etc. Bet poor Miss Daniel is busy evacuating children, etc. Here, apart from the gasmasks, they are digging trenches in the Quarry. Most things seem normal.

The reference to Muriel is one of only two in this diary to the future Mrs Wain. It must have been at about this time that, as she recalled some thirty years later, they walked down the street together, discussing the difficulty of getting pets into the anti-gas bags provided for them – such as Tiger, referred to above.

Thursday. Michaelmas Day

About 20 at mass – but then, they <u>do</u> turn up on Saints' Days. Day school before going to Lichfield. To get the name Michaelmas from the children, I pointed to a jar of mixed flowers & said "What do you call these flowers?" – & the only answer (a loud one) was "Dahlias!"

On the 10.55 I met the Thomas's all saying goodbye to Fred (R.A.F. exam in London) & travelled with him as far as W'hampton. Lunch with L.E.W.F. [*Luke Freeman*] at their house, & a walk in the Arboretum, then tea & to Lichfield – he came too & we met Creears at the station. Last year's gang [*i.e. those ordained deacon at the same time as FW, and now about to be ordained priest together*] were there (10) and 4 deacons-to-be. At the Palace they were as usual in confusion. The butler said "Well sir, we 'aven't quite decided w'ere to put you yet, sir." Up came the chaplain (Fred) [*Fred Chapman, Domestic and Diocesan chaplain to the Bishop of Lichfield since 1937.*] & said, "Oh, Mr Wain will have to be in The Palace after all", & up sailed the Bishopess with "Oh Mr Wain, AYME SHORE you wouldn't maynde being in what we call the Nursery, <u>would</u> you!" So when I'd feigned [*altered from* expressed] delight at the prospect, the butler took me away to show me the lavatories (as though I didn't know!) and said "Ye see sir, it's now [*sic*] good taking any notice of 'er, sir, or you'd be in the devil of a mess, see?" So I'm in a room right at the top of the building, where there's only gas light, labelled on the door "Bishop Butler, 1836". [*It is fascinating to speculate in which room this might have been. It is presumably now a school dormitory – but it has proved impossible to identify it.*]

Talked to the Bish [*Edward Woods, Bishop of Lichfield from 1937*] at supper – opposite was a protestant-looking fellow with a small moustache(!) who hadn't turned East for the Creed at Evensong. But it appears he is an ex-Baptist, so can be excused a lot – married, with 3 children, very brainy (Assyriology etc) – & a charming sort of person. Sorry for him. He had a couple of terms at Westcott House. The Retreat Conductor is Canon B. K. Cunningham of Westcott House, & he is very good – such a change from last year – devotional, & partly Catholic. He began tonight by saying "This is not a retreat" (it is not so-called this year – quite rightly) & explained how 2 Retreats wd be too much – for those who've had one, & the others [who] ought to have done! 2ndly he said he would be available for confessions! Quite open about it.

The concept of a retreat developed during the Counter-Reformation, and was introduced to the Church of England by the Tractarians, the first formal retreat being held at Oxford in 1856. Westcott House was – and is – a leading theological college at Cambridge, liberal catholic in stance. B K Cunningham, principal from 1919 to 1944, was described by Cyril Garbett, the contemporary Archbishop of York, as one of the two most influential men in the Church of England in his day (together with J B Seaton, the principal of Cuddesdon).

The Bish also gave an address – good. Also, what a treat it is to hear him read the Lesson again – he reads so well. My attitude to the Bish has quite changed. I like him immensely. I was so sorry for him, when he was pretending to remember us from last year, in the hall – no doubt he would remember the faces, but why try to do more, at his age & in his position? He is an excellent representative of his school – and what a fine Catholic he would have made! One's heart aches for him – misunderstood by those who should love him best, to say the least. Long may he reign.

This paragraph should perhaps be set against the disrespectful remarks in the entries for July 15th and 19th above! Bishop Woods' *Times* obituary (12th January, 1953) – not, of course, especially in that period, the place for hostile criticism – described him as "a man of deep, simple and sincere piety, ...extraordinarily persuasive in the difficult area of religious broadcasting, ... universally beloved by clergy and laity alike". It also says: "At Lichfield...he was an assuager of controversies, directing the minds of all to the great tasks of religious education...and above all of evangelism."

How weird this form of Compline is – Cunningham compiled it. Also I shall get a copy of the "Evangelical Group Movet [*Movement*]". [*Not clear what is meant – this is the name of a publishing house which published pamphlets rather than the title of a particular work.*]

Prayers we use – they only require a <u>little</u> discretion in using. Beautifully personal – too much so of course, but beautifully so.

Friday 30th September

Holy Communion said by the Bp very reverently, in a cope. At M & E'g [*Mattins and Evensong*] we are having the correct Psalms & Lessons this year. A.V. with R.V. interpolations occasionally [*Authorised (King James) Version with Revised Version interpolations*] And the 1928 prayer for the Ch. [*The 1928 Prayer Book was passed by Convocations and the Church Assembly, but rejected by the House of Commons after ultra-Protestant agitation, on the grounds that it was a betrayal of the Reformation, though in fact it also failed to satisfy the more advanced members of the High Church Party. It was widely, though unofficially, used up to the 1960s.*] Must tell our Mr Lee that the Bp himself does not say "militant here in earth"! [*The prayer referred to is the prayer of intercession at the Communion service, which in the 1662 BCP is introduced by the phrase "Let us pray for the whole state of Christ's Church militant here on earth". The omission of the last phrase in the 1928 book implies that you are also praying for the church expectant in Purgatory – a relatively 'advanced' idea!*] Intercessions again better than last year – by B.K. [*i.e. Cunningham*] – at 12.45, with ref to the crisis. And at lunch the Bish told us the wireless news – the 4 powers (Ch, H, Muss. & Deladier) have reached a satis'y agreement – dividing up Czechoa. A sort of revision, as it shd have been done at Versailles. All is well, glory be to God. If only Hitler is now content, & would at least tolerate Xnity.

BK very good in pointing out the strife between the opposing forces of good & evil in the universe – Michaelmas so appropriate. A victory for Michael & his Angels.

Chamberlain gave Hitler all that he had demanded at Godesberg the previous week. This was the day he returned to Downing Street, waving his piece of paper and predicting "Peace for our time". The relief shown in this diary was, of course, very widely felt – we who know what was going to happen the following year find it hard to share it. FW's reaction brings uncomfortable associations with Martin Niemoller's famous words:

"First they came for the Communists, and I did not speak up, because I was not a Communist. Then they came for the Jews, and I did not speak up, because I was not a Jew. Then they came for the Catholics, and I did not speak up, because I was a Protestant. Then they came for me, and by that time there was no one left to speak up for me."

FW continued:

Oaths etc postponed till tomorrow, as the Bish & family are going to London, Sat. midday, to see Robin ordained.

Bishop Woods' son, Robert, was ordained deacon in 1938. This is why FW was ordained priest by the Bishop of Stafford, Douglas Crick, though he had been ordained deacon the previous year by the diocesan bishop. Bishop Crick had been Bishop of Stafford since 1934 and Rector, since 1935, of

Edgmond – the same parish where FW was to serve as curate between 1951 and 1954. In 1939 Crick was promoted to the diocese of Chester. Robin Woods was eventually bishop of Worcester, 1971-1981.

> I've caught a rotten cold – partly thro' hurrying yesterday & partly through the Palace – & the Chapel certainly doesn't improve it. Coffee with Hemmings at the little place in Dam St. this morning. Yesterday a cup of tea with Holt & Creears at the Minster Café, where we met Mr & Mrs Cookson, quite a treat. Paid ordination fees in Murray Atkins' little office (which used to be stables) after tea. Raining hard all day, so this, & the pc's to the boys at Shrewsbury, had to be in the rain, which didn't improve my cold. But the Close, & the cathedral, in the rain quite romantic. Old times – Mr Hart etc., & last year – Bobby Timms & [?]Ganter. [*Added:*] Nobody but me dreams of putting out the various gaslights in the corridors at the top of the house!

Saturday 1st October

> B.K. said the Mass this morning – wouldn't use the cope, Canons of 1604 or not! Surplice & stole, quite nice.

The canons of 1604 are the principal body of canon law governing the Church of England since the Reformation. They dealt with a variety of subjects, of which one was the conduct of divine service. The cope is the semi-circular cloak, which Canon 24 ordered to be worn in cathedral and collegiate churches. It had been little used, but had been revived since the mid-nineteenth century.

At meals we have been reading Mackay's *Saints and leaders* – first Doc Johnson, then somebody else, then Frank Weston. [*By the Revd H F B Mackay, London, Allan, 1928. Dr Johnson, apart from his literary fame, was an staunch High Churchman, and was obviously appropriate to read about in Lichfield. Frank Weston was consecrated Bishop of Zanzibar in 1908, and lived amongst the Africans as one of themselves in a way that was well ahead of his time. At the second Anglo-Catholic Congress in 1923, where he was chairman, he made the oft-quoted warning: 'You cannot claim to worship Jesus in the Tabernacle if you do not pity Jesus in the slums...'.*] The Bish didn't know it, & asked B.K. to recommend chapter – typical of him – "comprehensive" [*means "Broad Church" in this context*] etc. When the chaplain was reading last night Mrs Bishop rose with dignity – I thought she was going to stop him reading about Benediction, but no – she was going to give them <u>all</u> a rest, & read herself – stumbling over words like Ponti-pont-igh-Pontifical! (Hooray).

High Mass – very valiant. How she told Creears "<u>We</u> clergy must keep fit" – "it behoves we clergy..." Apparently they both go for a run round the garden before breakfast – but tho' we've kept a look out we haven't seen them. During the morning Creears & I met Mr Banks of QM [*Queen Mary's Grammar School, Walsall*] in the Cathedral – another treat – & he capped this with a story of the vicar's wife who said "You know, <u>we</u> are the successors of the Apostles!"

At lunch the Bish said "We'll talk at this meal, chaps" & we did. Gabrielle [*the Bishop's daughter*] turned up again – I forgot to say Creears & Holt & I talked to her at coffee after dinner the first evening, & are quite convinced she is batty. And who wouldn't be, living in such a household – & with those brothers! She has a definite anti-parson complex. Poor kid. Painted finger nails & very slim. The Bish hurried off to London after lunch, forgetting his notes for a broadcast address – so the chaplain had to catch a train to B'ham to give him them, so the rehearsal of tomorrow's ceremonies had to be postponed till evening.

Gabrielle was twenty-two at this time, and had already been propositioned by Augustus John and studied sheep-farming in New Zealand. Batty or not, she had a distinguished future career (her married name was Pike) as Chairman of the National Federation of Women's Institutes (1961-1966), as a member of several government committees, and as a JP: she was appointed CBE in 1966. It would be fair to say that many products of clerical households would be seen as 'batty' by some – and a number develop an anti-parson complex! Her *Times* obituary (1st December, 1999) says that "her childhood was blissfully happy, though it is said that she did not always abide by school rules". Amongst her brothers, several were to attain high ecclesiastical office. Frank became Archbishop of Melbourne and Primate of Australia, Robin Bishop of Worcester [see above under 30th September], and Samuel Archdeacon of Christchurch, New Zealand. An uncle was Bishop of Winchester.

Before lunch (& oaths) I had my interview. The Bish, as usual very charming – called me Young Wain. I told him about school chaplaincy, & he made a note of it & said he might find something in a few years' time.

Would I prefer a Woodard School or a normal public school? "They need you so much, you know!" I'm afraid I haven't given him quite a fair impression of how definitely Catholic I am. Still, we did have a talk (he said "Then are you a <u>rigid</u> Catholic?" & I said "It depends what you mean by that!"). I think so much of the C of E – it is true that it is as he says "glorious", tho' we feel fed up at times. Pr'aps I ought to have told him I signed the C.U. [*Church Union*] statement. But I certainly see nothing wrong in keeping on good terms with him, as I'm afraid some haven't.

The Woodard schools were a group of public schools with a marked Anglo-Catholic ethos, founded by Nathaniel Woodard, beginning in 1848. The first and best known is Lancing, but others include Hurstpierpoint, Bloxham, Prestfelde, Denstone and Worksop. They were described by Desmond Morse-Boycott, *The secret story of the Oxford Movement*, as "an effectual means of catholicising the Middle Classes".

Interview with the Archdeacon (Stafford) at 7.15 tonight, very invigorating – Confession – instruction in saying Mass – parish chapter meetings – visiting, etc. A great man.

Have got some quinine for my cold, which has already worked wonders. Met L.E.W.F. in Dam St, just before. He is back from Cambridge, but the pain under his arm is an abscess, which has to be lanced, & then frequently dressed, so he may not be able to come to Sh'y for my first Mass, nor even to the Ordination. Very good letter by the way from Frs Symonds [*CR*] & Heanney. What a number of these fellows have already married (or engaged) (mentioning it to the Bish too). But they are mostly so old. Scarcely any ascetic ideals – but who am I to criticise?

No tea at the Palace tomorrow after all, in the absence of the family, so it is just as well I delayed asking anybody. Only 2 breakfasts & 2 cups of tea tomorrow, out of 14 – not as bad as last year – notice for noughts & crosses on the Library door. (The "Great Hall" now called the Library by the way).

The point of this is that ten out of the fourteen candidates intended to keep the Eucharistic fast – no food or drink before Communion from the previous midnight. This "ancient and laudable custom" (in the words of the 1928 Prayer Book) had almost died out in the C of E in the eighteenth century, and been revived by the Tractarians.

A doss this afternoon instead of a walk (weather cleared up with the political situation) – how good it wd have been to watch the big trains. Glad to find the new Bish keeps up the custom of the old one in watching the trains!

All this is very full this year, since I wrote practically nothing last time. One more thing & then bed. The usual business of asking us not to do Catholic things, for the sake of uniformity. We bow instead of kneeling at the *Incarnatus* (use of pre-Reformation Exeter only!) – but this time they ask for no genuflections after Communion – well, they will get 'em – from 7 or 8 of us. It is in an entirely different category, & one would not dream of giving way.

The *Incarnatus* is the "And was incarnate for us by the Holy Ghost of the Virgin Mary" phrase in the Nicene Creed. Different customs prevailed on this, even within the Anglo-Catholic tradition. The bow at this point is founded in the Old English (Sarum) rite; the genuflexion in the Modern (Roman) rite. See also below under 4th October. FW's elder son remembers them bowing at this phrase at Lichfield Cathedral in the 1960s, but at Shrewsbury Abbey the custom was to kneel. A "use" is the local modification of a standard liturgical rite, of which there were a number in the Middle Ages.

The two fellows who weren't accustomed to turning East for the creed have fallen into line since the first Evensong. Last year 2 even asked to be priested without stoles [*a liturgical vestment like a scarf, worn by the deacon like a sash over the left shoulder and by the priest round the neck*] – & got away with it! This year the Archdeacon is going to change our stoles from Deacon– to Priest–wise. He said, by the way, that he wd love to start a school for vicars "How to train deacons"! And that I must have time for Retreat in addition to the holiday. The Gospeller is a Lichfield man – a very quiet person, don't know how he will get on – but I expect they said the same about me.

[*Added at top of page*: The rehearsal (like other things) most inefficient. But the meals not late, as last year.]

Though it looks like 10.45, I know it is only 9.45, so a hot bath, some more quinine & bed.

SUNDAY, TRINITY X, October 2, 1938

What on earth to write about such a wonderful day? Best to put it down as it happened.

At 8.30 I lay warmly in bed, thinking of the boys starting out from Sh'y in the pouring rain. It was absolutely pelting down.

9.30 Mattins in the Palace Chapel, & 10.15 we gathered in the common Room – the rain cleared just enough to let us process into the Cathedral – the usual few sightseers awe-stricken by the unexpected sight. The Bp (Douglas – Stafford) was most impressive, being so tall, in cope & mitre & with 2 choirboys in red cassocks to butterfly his cope. Procn round the nave with *Come Thou Holy Spirit, Come* (A&M), [*156 in the Standard Edition*] & I noticed much fewer friends, owing to the bad weather. But this meant it was much less of a strain afterwards, greeting them. At the front of the Nave were David Selby, Ted Everton, Howard Smith & his wife – & somewhere Miss Wedge & MRS STEVENS – she unexpected of course, but what a dear saintly person of the old school! I didn't know until she came up afterwards, in the rain, with tears in her eyes. The sermon: fortunately only half the length of last year's (but nearly 20 mins), & BK wasn't half as good as one expected after the earlier addresses – but good all the same, for those who could hear! He said afterwards that he'd never preached to a pillar before – nor on such an elevated perch! Then led by the Archdeacon & presented in the Sanctuary. Somewhere up here was Mrs Freeman, but I didn't notice her –

and in the North Choir aisle, God bless them, Tony Lovell, Ray Davies, John Cox, Bill Woodnorth & Tom Brown – arrived safely! Tony announced later that the service was Ireland, & the Agnus & Benedictus Merbecke – certainly I sh'dn't have distinguished them, tho' I knew it was something we know. I was the first to be ordained priest, & I mustn't write anything about it, except the word – wonderful. And the Bp clasped our hands in delivering the Bible. It was news to me that he couldn't sing – he intoned the preface etc on one note, & in this respect last year was better. They had shortened the service in one or two respects – eg the Litany, & what I didn't like so much, we replied to the Bp's questions all together instead of one by one.

Several incidents stand out – 1st, as last year, returning from the choir – the vast sweep of the Cathedral roof – but no sunlight this time – then turning up to go to the Chapter House, with the boys eagerly looking round. [*From the North Choir aisle they would have had a good view of that!*] Here we were given letters of orders (no Sunday School prizegiving this year) & as they hadn't been signed, it took some time. The Bp spoke about Judith Butts [*see above, entry for September 16th*] – he seemed to know each one, tho' he is only suffragan. Just outside the choir L.E.W.F. was waiting – & insisted on paying for lunch! Then outside the North door – the boys – Tony was just inside the porch, & the others at the top of the steps. They did give me a welcome – they'd been awfully thrilled.

Lunch all together at the Minster Café. It was a great joy to have them with me, tremendous happiness –

Give thanks to God for my

Ordination to the Priesthood

by

BISHOP DOUGLAS CRICK

in Lichfield Cathedral

and my

First Holy Mass

in the Abbey Church,

Shrewsbury,

October 2nd and 4th, 1938.

———

FRANK WAIN.

———

"Holy Father, in union with Mary I offer Jesus to you, and I offer myself with Him, with all His intentions, and in the name of all His creatures."

B.O. & W.   LONDON, E.C.

TIBI LAUS TIBI GLORIA TIBI GRATIARUM ACTIO

SANCTUS

SANCTUS   SANCTUS

SACRIFICIŪ   NOSTRUM
ASCENDAT   AD TE DÑE
ET DESCENDAT   SUPER NOS
MISERICOR   DIA TUA

Abbaye de Maredret S.M 15   Made in Belgium

indeed the whole day – so much sheer joy in one day is too much. Fortunately it only happens twice in a lifetime – I really think today was more so than last year. Showed them all round the cathedral – all the interesting things I love.

When I fetched my things from the Palace, I took Tony in – knowing we shouldn't meet anybody important. In the Great Hall (or "Library"), one of the fellows asked "Is that your brother?" In all honesty, for the moment, the reply ought to have been, "No, but he half wishes he was!" I've never seen boys so full of joy. Saw them off at the west end just before Evensong (at 4). The BELLS! All afternoon – and just then they began <u>crashing</u>, as I call it – all ringing nearly simultaneously – then they broke into a peal again – in the most perfect control. I think there are ten. [*This is correct – they were founded in 1688, to replace those destroyed in the Civil War.*] It began to spot with rain again, just as they were sardining themselves into the car. And so off.

Evensong was very good – a thanksgiving for the crisis being over – deliverance from the dreadful shadow of war. But I couldn't help making it more of a thanksgiving for <u>my day</u> – and all the happiness. We began with *Now thank we all our God* – but couldn't compete with the organ: Ambrose Porter [*organist at the Cathedral from 1925 to 1959*] at the organ is as magnificent as ever – if you like organs. But it's hard luck on the choir! We were sitting in the North transept, as the Mayor & Corporation were in the South, so we got the full blast. I was waiting for the terrific trumpet stop I heard once, but it never came. The Bp's butler, & wife, & the cook, etc., were close by.

The Dean read the first lesson, & we, a couple of yards away, could just about hear him – no doubt we shall never hear him again (but I've been saying this for a long while!). [*Henry Erwin Savage took office in 1909; he died in 1939.*] Canon Stockley read the 2nd Lesson [*either Matthew ch. 6, or Luke ch. 11*], & in it the Our Father came – there was a movement in choir – & lo! they keep up the old tradition of standing for it. So I stood too, but none of the others. From the sound, I shd think most of the Nave did too. I think when you come to a place where they observe these old customs, you ought to back them up. The Bishop (Stafford) preached – he was supposed to be 5 mins only, but took 15 – & was very surprised, afterwards, to hear it!

Then they sang *O God our help*, while we were vergered up the choir aisle to the sanctuary – getting a full view of those <u>gorgeous</u> choirmen, lounging against the stalls! The canons had put on 6 of the loveliest copes I've ever seen, & we had a really beautiful mediaeval procession, the Bp bringing up the rear in cope & mitre. Everything except incense! But my word it was good. The nave & S. transept were packed as I've never seen them – crowds standing at the west end. Going down I noticed Mr Merrett of QM – of all people (tho' I ought not to be surprised) – & grinned at him. It was impossible to do otherwise. Coming up the centre aisle, we reserved a couple of verses of the hymn for entering the choir, & the organist played part of the Hallelujah

Chorus. It was truly magnificent. Then, all grouped in the Sanctuary (& us!). The choir sang Martin's *Te Deum* (in C?). Anyway it was jolly good – but I fancy the Abbey <u>boys</u> sing better. But p'raps they are inclined to shout – & again, they haven't that perfect purity of tone. Also they haven't the same competition from the organ!

Tea with Holt, Howell, the ex-Baptist & another, at the *George*. Mr Merrett & a new master at QM were also there.

B.K. was good at 7.30 – he just read a little of the discourses in S. John to us. [*Presumably part of John chs. 14-16.*] "Now you poor dears have been on your knees long enough today. You are not to do any more praying." How perfectly understanding! He also read *The Priest's Prayer to Jesus*. At supper I talked to Chapman the chaplain (the Inefficient) – he has actually begun calling us by our Xn names. Compline was cancelled, & we have been chatting by the fire in the "Library" since supper.

Monday 3rd October

[*Added at top of page*: I shd have mentioned Cecil Sayer sent me a copy of Evelyn Underhill's *Worship* – and Miss Daniel is sending a book.] Taxi – & to Walsall with Hemmings, Whitehouse & another. They went on of course. Lunch with L.E.W.F. – who definitely can't come to Sh'y. Bussing it to W'hampton for the sake of the extra few minutes, I should have missed the G.W.R. train, had it not been 10 mins late.

As usual I found in the compartment a large selection
of the day's papers!! Well…Czechoslovakia is going
to be divided up – & they are all thanking them for
allowing themselves to be sacrificed! Most ironic of
all is the way the German people hail Hitler as the
preserver of peace! A few people have been killed by
A.R.P. trenches falling in, & a few have tried out their
gasmasks with ordinary domestic gas, & car engine
exhausts, with lamentable results – one or two have
even succeeded in committing suicide with them!

The Times, which was evidently FW's normal newspaper
is often regarded as the mouthpiece of the Appeasement policy,
because the editor, Geoffrey Dawson, had a close political
relationship with Chamberlain, but there is certainly no hint
in this diary that FW was aware of its bias, nor of the existence
of an alternative stance. No doubt most of the public were
simply glad to have been spared war, and were not too critical
of the details of the policy which had averted it.

R M Barrington-Ward, the deputy-editor of *The Times*,
wrote a letter to a private correspondent on 4th October, the
following day, which casts an interesting light on the remark
about people thanking the Czechs:

Admiration for the coolness and restraint which Benesh
has so wisely shown in these last few weeks is one thing.
'Gratitude' is another. I am sorry for him, but I am
not grateful to him. I regard him…as one of the most
active architects of disorder in Europe.

The House of Commons debated the Munich settlement
from 3rd to 6th October. According to Churchill, "the German
dictator, instead of snatching the victuals from the table, has

been content to have them served to him course by course". In withering tones, he pointed out that the Czechs could have secured terms as good as Chamberlain had brought back without British intervention at any time during the summer. "Silent, mournful, abandoned, broken, Czechoslovakia recedes into the darkness. She has suffered in every respect from her association with the Western democracies and with the League of Nations, of which she has always been an obedient servant...." All too accurately, he predicted that the rest of Czechoslovakia would not retain her independence long. Thirty Conservatives abstained at the end of the debate, and Duff Cooper, the First Lord of the Admiralty, resigned from the Government.

Back in the pouring rain to find a huge mail awaiting me! Ordination letters of course – and Exhibn ones too – now we're glad we didn't abandon it. The numbers of children have risen to nearly 800. A lovely letter from Audrey. I sent her an enlargement of the Walsingham snap – and her family think I'm very nice. Apparently she has a father, mother, 2 brothers & one sister.

A good "Africa" Rehearsal, for which we got the vestments out, but the censer has been loaned to S. Mary's. Young produced his biretta for indoor use! Miss Ormiston whispered that she wd be there tomorrow – & I had a charming letter from old Mrs Mackay, who hopes to come too. Tony & Ray came in afterwards. Ray hasn't made his Communion since he left the orphanage, but is going to turn over a new leaf tomorrow (let us hope so anyway, & pray).

Tuesday 4th October, S. Francis

What can one write about the first Mass? It was a great joy. The howling gale prevented Mrs M. & Miss O. (so old) from coming, & Mrs Green & Mrs MacNabb were away. Young served. There were 12 in spite of the weather – including Barbara Elliott & Miss Myott, the Vicar & Mrs W, Tony, Ray & Bill. A Holy Spirit Mass: Canon: S. Francis & Trinity XIV. I think the worst moment was the beginning of the Preparation – mind a blank – would I remember even that? [*The private prayers said before the opening of the service as given in the BCP. The section begins with Psalm 43.*] Then all went well – but I was very slow. No one was more surprised than me to hear the clock strike 8! It's the private prayers that take the time – henceforth, I shall use the English Canon, with the appropriate actions – I can't think the other is worth it! [I.*e. he suggests that the simpler English rite – based on mediaeval usage – is preferable to the more elaborate Western – Roman – rite.*] Lumley, this afternoon (when I went to borrow the censer back, & met the new curate – the one who said Mass the day I went back to Mirfield) – Lumley said his first Mass took well over half an hour. I had the censer in order to show John Cox how! And incidentally to give the Abbey a really good fumigation.

This afternoon I cast religion & the Exhibition aside – & saw Robert Taylor in *A Yank at Oxford* (at the Granada). Do the women still fall for him? Personally I loathed him from start to finish. [*This film was made in 1938. Also in it were Maureen O'Sullivan, Vivien Leigh and Lionel Barrymore. Taylor was later a "friendly witness" during the McCarthyite House Un-American Activities Committee investigation of Hollywood.*]

Mrs Brett writes that she can't hear mass for me today, as there isn't one where she is staying. And on Sunday they had a remarkable do – not antecommunion, but the <u>latter half</u> of the Mass, after Choral Mattins – & the priest said the Consecration Prayer with his legs wide apart, & his hands behind his back! Then he took up the Paten [*the dish with the bread on it*] with one hand, turned round to face the congregation and laid his other hand upon it as he said the words! Now she knows what her remark, "Protestant Mass", really means!…

Wednesday 5th October

Yesterday Miss Ormiston asked for my blessing when she called to see me. At Mass I only gave one – to Young – the boys were too shy to come up alone, & the Thomas's weren't there.

Today: Mass at Prestfelde 7.30 and to the Music Hall to help prepare for the Exhibition, at 9 o/c. There all day. The show promises to be good – but the British Workmen who put up the stage were just too typically British – & Salopian! S. Mary's dress rehearsal for the play not at all bad – but our first hymn could have been a better choice – & all our singing unaccompanied. If their boy doesn't stop coughing – all the prots in the congregation will say "Oh that poor child". Their thurifer a nice fellow – awfully anxious about the incense!

Thursday 6th October

All day & every day, a dreadful rush. Sermon for Pitchford Harvest not ready yet! [*Pitchford was a village five miles from Shrewsbury. See below, entry for October 9th.*] It's definitely a jolly good show – especially the conversion scenes at the end – people saying "how lovely" etc. Mostyn & Ray turned up & were pleased to be roped in as stewards. The incense goes well, now that the boy has at last absorbed my instructions that the charcoal has jolly well <u>got</u> to be red-hot & plenty of it. We dealt with 123 children – it will be 1,000 before the end of the show. Ray may start serving Tuesdays. Peter Ford made valiant use of his season ticket by turning up tonight! Day school – the babies' harvest festival: I told 'em about naughty Tommy Brown who didn't like Harvest festivals – they hooted derision – cdn't believe such a monstrous child existed!!

Friday 7th October

Similar, except that I carefully stayed away from the Exhibn except when I was needed. The headmaster of Shrewsbury was the opener [*i.e. of Shrewsbury School, the ancient public school. The headmaster from 1932-44 was Henry Harrison Hardy. For more on the school, see below, entry for 12th October.*], & Mr Dovey [*headmaster of Prestefelde*] chairman – both good. Came away after the children's session, met Ronald Clint – who came in for a long talk – it was <u>practically</u> a confirmation class!

Saturday 8th October

Said Mass again today. Up go the numbers of children for the last few days – we shall have a dreadful time, with nearly 300 each night. The Bishop of the Diocese opened this afternoon – his speech was very good. Came & chatted to Rawlins & me, & Lumley. Met "Dickie" on my way there – he fears the scouts will have to close down (I've not been for ages). There's some trouble about not being able to afford to pay the rent. Tonight Tony & Ray came to the Exhibition, & stayed to see how S. Mary's do the conversion scenes (actually they do them very well) and we all had refreshments (plus Alan Rickard) & all was very nice! Back home on the bus.

Midday I walked home with Mrs Walker, stopping every few seconds for her to get her breath, while she told me how they had all had their gasmasks in the Alms houses – the old darling said "I hear as they're going to bring round <u>cartoons</u> to keep 'em in. I put mine in an old shoebox."

Now the crisis was over, there were many jokes about gas-masks. Several were told by "An Air Raid Warden" in that week's *Shrewsbury Chronicle*. (*Sermons in gas masks; how Shrewsbury met the crisis.*) One tells of a "good-looking flapper" who put on a mask, struck a pose and asked how she looked. She was "terribly peeved" to be told that she looked like a prehistoric monster. Another tells of the housewife who said "This is the sort of thing we ought to wear when peeling onions."

Sunday – Trinity XVII

Assisted at 8 o/c & said the children's Mass. Breakfast, & then I came in for 11 o/c – for several reasons. Mr Howard (of UMCA [*Universities' Mission to Central Africa*]) preached, & was very good, but he failed to interest some of our confounded choirmen – or Alan Young, who talked from beginning to end of the Mass. Then I gave Ray Hotchkiss a serving rehearsal – & a little instruction. He said "Well that's different from what I learned at school" – so what!!

The Dress Rehearsal for the play was held this afternoon at the Music Hall – pretty bad. However, they got roundly told off for not bowing at the Holy Name and to the Altar.... . Fr Hambling says that when he came to the Abbey to preach he thought they were the most irreverent choir he'd ever met. I told him they are far worse in the morning! However, it's quite true that they are better than they used to be.

Alan Young has appeared in the cast in place of Dennis Grivell – my hat, he's going to have to watch his step. Miss Ormiston, kind lady, is treating all the boys to tea tomorrow. To Pitchford to preach at the Harvest Festival. Fr Stokes, the Vicar, fetched me in his car at 5.50. Miss Myatt & Auntie Annie came, & some of the boys biked over – including alas, Pat Thomas, who wants to leave the choir. There was a huge congregation for such a small church, & the decorations very tasteful – mostly flowers, very few vegetables. They have raised nearly £1200 to restore the roof (death-watch beetle). The other day Fr M said they have the death-watch beetle at S. Mary's.

Monday 10th October

A tremendous day at the Exhn – the Mothers' Union in great crowds all afternoon, and 349 children at 5.30. I was roped in to give an extra talk in the Church court, & managed quite decently. Mem – tomorrow not to grumble when they knock down the catachumen barrier – bessed article! It supplied the introduction for my talks! At tea met Fr Charles Edwards of Market Drayton – a good cove. He supplied what I've not heard before: CMS = Christianity Minus Sacraments! and SPG= Some Part of the Gospel! [*A disrespectful joke about two evangelical missionary societies. They are in fact, of course, the Church Missionary Society and the Society for the Propagation of the Gospel, founded respectively in 1799 and 1701. Later on, in 1947, Edwards became Vicar of St Martin in the Fields.*] Then our turn at doing the Conversion scenes – all went very well – a bad Dress Rehearsal meaning a good performance. But the way some people (eg Mrs W. [*i.e. Mrs Wilkinson, the Vicar's wife*]) get on everybody's nerves – well, honestly, thank God we aren't having another Nativity Play. It's very hard to keep detached. Miss O. [*Ormiston*] stood the boys tea, & they were very happy thoughout – came home on the bus with a few from the Monkmoor direction.

The *Shrewsbury Chronicle* carried a photograph of "The confirmation", one of the tableaux depicting "The conversion of the African" at the African Missionary Exhibition. Reproduction was not good enough to guess whether FW might have been on this!

Tuesday 11th October

Missed Mass – couldn't stir a muscle! Mislaid the crucifix Fr Hassall gave me – last night in the dressing room – hope to goodness I find it. Tea today with Mrs Vaughan, the layer out of corpses. Everything pretty much as usual, but not so many children.

Wednesday 12th October – last day

Sung Mass of Thanksgiving at S. Mary's. Fr M. [*Millington*] celebrant, Young & Mayhew served, Lumley & Fr Hambling cantors, Jack Rawlins & my Vicar & I, the choir. Quite a fair congregation. Found my crucifix in the Vicar's bag, where it had been put for safety – after I was blacked. [*Presumably made up for the play.*] Funeral this afternoon.

Then to the Exhn – a pretty good day. 219 children this afternoon. The performance equally good. How vastly superior to S Mary's our boys' voices are – several people commented, including Mrs Mackenzie. I wasn't required so much for talks – only twice. Young good with the magic lantern. Met Hopwell, headmaster of Monkmoor – also Mr Pugh, from there, an All Saints' man – both good – they announced it & brought 100 of the boys, though it's a Council school. It was some time before the boys spotted that Mr Howard's helpers were not really African! He accidentally addressed them in English!

The numbers at the children's sessions have been as follows: Thurs: 125. Fri: 162. Mon: 349. Tues: 284. Wed:

219 – making 1139 in all. Add 30 schoolgirls who paid 3d, not knowing of the special arrangements, and 250 at least from private schools at morning sessions, and you get about 1500, which is reckoned jolly good. None at all came from THE school – Fr Hambling said a few sarcastic things about HB being a leading A/C [*Anglo-Catholic*] , & doing nothing, but then <u>he</u> knows nothing of the terrific snobbishness in a place like that. They wouldn't touch a missionary Exhn with a barge pole, in spite of the Headmaster & the chaplain!!

See above, 7th October. HB is Humphrey Beevor, the school chaplain from 1937-41, who did indeed have the reputation of being High Church. A former Librarian at Pusey House, his later career took him to be editor of the *Church Times* (where one of his news editors was the future Prime Minister, Ted Heath) and eventually Bishop of Lebombo. The boys of the day are said to have chanted: "Humphrey Beevor/ is a great believer/ in Original Sin". For more on him, see below under October 24th.

Tomorrow clearing up the mess at the Music Hall & packing, and then – return to normal, thank goodness. But it's been very good fun, & well worth it. Back home by bus tonight, with one companion only, the inseparable – fidus Alwyn. [*"Fidus" means loyal – an allusion to the Aeneid Book 1, line 188, where the reference is to "Fidus Achates".*] Not nearly as tired as usual, but I shall be tomorrow! Cyril Cox is in the Eye, Ear & Throat – hope I manage to see him soon.

Thursday 13th October

Account in a paper of Leslie Weatherhead welcoming a colleague at the City Temple – a Woman Preacher (nomine [*by name*] Dorothy Wilson). "She used only one gesture throughout her sermon". "As a preacher Miss Wilson is the feminine counterpart of Dr Weatherhead". (!) "The two co-pastors are of the same age, 45. Both have been warned by their medical advisers against the dangers of overwork". Another female preacher writes of the effort: "I cannot express the feeling of exhilaration that fills me".

Leslie Weatherhead was an influential Methodist minister and author of the time. Theologically liberal, he was not the sort of minister for FW to find inspiring!

Sunday 16th October '38 (TRINITY XVIII)

A row after the Sung Mass this morning: The boys had been exceptionally quiet, really good – but the men made as much noise as boys and men put together usually do. So when passing through them to the priests' vestry, I foolishly remarked, "I hope you noticed, gentlemen, that the boys set you a very good example this morning". After a while in came Fred Holding in an awful temper – he must have been one of those talking during the Consecration.

As I only said the first (Holy Ghost) of a new priest's first three masses at the time, on Wednesday I said a Votive Mass of Our Lady, and today a Requiem. On Wed only Mrs Holden was present, and today only

Mrs MacNabb & Jim Braddock, who served. The Vicar returned this evening after a few days in Lincolnshire, and Rawlins & I came away early from a meeting of the SS Assoc, to see *The Invisible Man* at the King's. It was jolly good, I thought. [*Filmed in 1933, directed by James Whale, with Claude Rains as the Invisible Man.*]

Having been very fed up & depressed for about 3 weeks – or indeed since the holidays – I've now cheered up. Strange but true, how suddenly the change came! And the reason is fairly clear – spiritual life having gone to the dogs. Now I really mean to do something about it! – for the first time ever, I've begun preparing the meditation the evening before – & the difference it makes passes belief.

The chief thing now is to get into church before Mrs H begins cleaning! Every blessed day that woman clatters round the Abbey – she certainly ought to get saved by works! Also Mattins will jolly well have to be said before leaving the house from now on – there surely is no other parish where the clergy don't have a key to the church door – & old Bilcliffe can't be expected to let down the portcullis more than a quarter of an hour before Mass. Young gave me a copy of *Ritual Notes* this evening. He says that when the "Empire" is re-opened by the Mayor & Corporation on Monday night (after renovation) there is going to be a crowd of about 5000 protesting against the dismissal of the late Manager!

The copy of *Ritual Notes* still survives amongst FW's books. It is inscribed on the fly-leaf: *Frank Wain. In festa. Dom: xvii post Pentecost, 1938. dd. S.E.W.Y.* The date is, of course, the ordination day, 2nd October. (17th Sunday after Pentecost, 16th after Trinity), "*dd*" means *dedit* (he gave) and the initials are those of Stan Young. The book's full title is *Ritual notes; a comprehensive guide to the rites and ceremonies of the Book of Common Prayer of the English Church, interpreted in accordance with the recently revised "Western Use".* Compiled by Henry Cairncross and others. 8th edition, London, Knott, 1935.

Saturday 22nd October

The boys played All Saints' choir at football – pitch up by the Column – alas, we lost, 6-4 – but they all played magnificently, & it was a good game. [*The Column commemorates Lord Hill, 1772-1842, and is the tallest Doric column in the world.*] We borrowed a whistle from Spence's at the post office, & a Mr. James from All Saints' refereed very capably – made all the difference. At 7 o/c, to S. Chad's, to play their club at pingpong – Tony & Ray & Mostyn & Ray H. We won easily – but next time we must take some smaller fry – as their small boys are smaller than we expected. Rawlins & I arranged to go up to London at the beginning of December – I shall see Audrey – day excursion. What an idea, & strange that it never occurred to me before!

Sunday 23rd October

Didn't say Mass today – I wonder if it will happen again on a Sunday? Probably not, because of the new church. Y'see, we had Morning Prayer, with a large M.P., [*emphasising that it was a service of Mattins rather than of Communion*] for the Mayor & Corporation – who came to support the appeal for the Abbey Day School. The collection at Mattins was £14 odd – more than the total for last year. Congregation much larger – the Rector of Wem preached – I shd say a good preacher – too much poetry in it – but it was good stuff, Noyes & others.

Alfred Noyes, 1880-1958, was a poet. His best-known works included one called *The highwayman*, and one called *The barrel organ* which has the refrain "Go down to Kew in lilac-time, in lilac-time, in lilac-time…". In 1927 he became a Roman Catholic and he published a book of theological essays.

The choir sang Stanford's *Te Deum* magnificently, & the Day School were there in full force. A bevy of policemen in the south aisle were bored stiff. Imagine them, in a Catholic country, all taking their proper part in the Mass. Fr Roach came, as Mayor's Chaplain, to find his places for him, as he said, leaving Rawlins with the whole burden of S. Chad's & the barracks on his shoulders, & no breakfast till lunch!

Talked to the Bible Class before Sunday School – about the Mass – not a very good attendance because they all thought there was no class in Mr Adams' absence. Three baptisms this afternoon, but fortunately Young took them – one baby squawled loudly from beginning to end. Afterwards a strange little girl in a red hat told me she was going to have jelly for tea.

Sang Evensong – Vicar preached, very boring. Ray Davies, Fred Thomas & Eric Hughes were in the congregation, but not Colin (Robert being home on leave!).

Monday 24th October

Said Mass at 11 o/c – far too late for a weekday! Headache all day as a result. A sort of conference with the Bish, in S. Mary's hall. Followed by tea & a few prayers in the church. Met a few priests unknown till now. McCarthy & the aged Ingrams were there from the Schools. [*Shrewsbury School (see above, 7th October), is often referred to as "The Schools". The Rev F L McCarthy, who later became Chaplain of Balliol College, Oxford, was on the staff from 1933 to 1945. F M Ingram had been a housemaster from 1908 to 1929.*] The old man wasn't any too pleased at the changes Fr Beevor has made up there, but glad to hear he is a "great favourite with the boys". P'raps he's managed to introduce wafer bread! [*An Anglo-Catholic practice.*] More likely to know what's good for 'em than this old dear! For the second time I've heard the Catholic Religion referred to as a "groove" – as if the other thing wasn't an infinitely worse groove.

Bishop and Mrs Woods were in Shrewsbury together. On the Tuesday she opened a sale of work in aid of the Home Missionary Society at St Mary's Hall. On the Sunday he had preached for St Mary's Dedication Festival. His sermon was reported in some detail in the *Chronicle*, including the sentence: "The church did not say to a man 'You are black' or 'You are the citizen of a great Empire' but 'You are a child of God and Jesus Christ died for you'."

Wednesday, 26th October

With Rawlins to see Will Hay in *Convict 99* at the Granada – not as good as *Oh Mr Porter*.

Convict 99 was a 1938 comedy in which Will Hay played a schoolmaster who applied for a job in a prison, where he was taken first for a prisoner, then for the governor. It also starred Moore Marriott and Googie Withers. *Oh Mr Porter* was made earlier the same year and had many of the same actors in; it was a story of an incompetent stationmaster posted to an apparently haunted station in Northern Ireland, where he met a ruthless gang of gun-runners.

Tea at Morris's. He says when the Bish met the church councillors, etc., Mon evening, Mrs Bird wanted to know why he only preached from one pulpit in the town! [*Presumably the wife of the Vicar of All Saints!*]

Thursday 27th October

Talked to John Altrey after Mass – said by Young in a purple vestment, for the vigil, which didn't exactly "go" with the blue frontal & John Cox's red cassock, to say nothing of the carpet. Altrey (if his name is John) is only a kid after all, & has had a year at Kelham, which he has just left, after deciding he hasn't a vocation. Went to Ellesmere College [*one of the Woodard schools, in Shropshire*], where Fr Sharpe persuaded him to try Kelham.

This afternoon the Russian choir, at S. Mary's, were awfully good. Quite a crowd, & I shd imagine a <u>very</u>

good collection, including some £1 notes. From 6-8 this evening an A.R.P. "Blackout". This was very interesting, & good fun, but not exciting. We blocked up the windows, finding the shutters wd work, & then popped out from time to time to see what was happening. Mr Lakier was at the corner of Monkmoor Rd, thoroughly enjoying himself, like a boy scout.

The *Chronicle* commented: "It was a bold step to arrange the black out so early in the evening, with traffic on the move and need for light in every home, but the hours chosen provided a much fairer test of what can be done than an exercise at midnight, which has been the practice at other places." The blackout covered an area of 400 square miles, and wardens met motorists at the boundaries of the area and told them to drive on side-lights. Footpaths and traffic islands were picked out in white or marked with red lamps. There were throngs of people in the town centre enjoying the novelty. There was a practice mobilisation of ARP personnel and vehicles; "mild explosions...added a note of realism".

28 October '38. S. Simon & S. Jude – FOUNDATION DAY at Mirfield.

Said Mass at 7.30 & sent a telegram just before lunch, remembering just in time! Letter from Audrey – when I go on an excursion to London she is going to get the day off!

The Bp of London *[Arthur Winnington-Ingram, at that see since 1901]* preaching tonight at S. Mary's – (how live they have become – Mahew has been writing to the *Ch Times* about the Rosary!) Huge crowds tonight, as all through their dedication Festival – very well advertised. I missed Rawlins, but got invited into the choir instead. In the vestry the dear old Bishop remembered coming to Leeds years ago, & spoke about Fr Biggart. Also he said "The dear old Abbey…". Then we had Evensong, my second tonight. Their choir may sing badly but they're very reverent. The effect of the alterations in the lighting of the sanctuary is very good. The Rural Dean, Renfree, Mahew & I were in choir, Lumley acted as chaplain. Rawlins & Young were in the congregation, where I saw them during the procession – also Dick Alder, who apparently came over from Nantwich.

Richard Alder had been at the College a year before FW, and was now a curate at Nantwich.

The Bp preached very simply, but for nearly three quarters of [*altered from* half] an hour. But nobody minded a bit. Afterwards he seemed tired, & a bit lost, but was most particular to say goodbye & God bless you to us – unfortunately I had to be called back! He made them laugh by saying he never preached so long when he was a curate. [*He had been a curate at that very church in 1885.*]

Saturday 29th October

Coffee with Rawlins & a friend of his at the old house in Butcher Row. This afternoon our boys played S. Giles' – but I didn't go till 3.30, & it was just as well – only 7 a side, & they were beaten 4-1 (or 2). A poor game. Up the Column with Alwyn – we had a good

view, & amused ourselves by spitting from the top –
then to tea with the Spences at the Column.

Sunday Trinity XX 1938

Hooray! I forgive everybody everything – I'm going
to have all the boys to prepare for confirmation!

Monday – Eve of All Saints'

Solemn Evensong & Procession at All Saints' – very
heartening indeed! Young & the Vicar & Rawlins &
Fr Butler came & a number of G.S.S. servers. [*Guild
of Servants of the Sanctuary – an association of altar servers
in the Church of England.*] Fr Beevor preached. Cecil
Gibbs came, & Mr Halford (two good blokes). A good
but quiet sermon – apparently Fr Bird [*Vicar of All
Saints*] is a very good preacher. Noticed quite a number
of young fellows & boys whom I'd often wondered
about, who, it turned out, belong to All Saints'. Tea
& cakes in their parish hall – quite a nice one. And
Mr Halford said "You know these people who complain
that the Abbey is High? Well, they don't know what
they're talking about!" Good for him! And it reminds
me I must go to B'ham & buy me a Lady statue. [*See
above, 24th August.*] Also I must start announcing the
text <u>before</u> the Invocation!

Wednesday 2nd November. ALL SOULS' DAY '38

Said Mass 9.30. How dumb our congregation are –
thro' the Vicar making the responses so loud – when
he ain't there, they won't do it! At the Working Party's

tea this afternoon, it turns out there is a rumour that the W's are leaving – even Mrs Mackay has asked "is it true?"!!! [*In fact he remained there for nearly twenty more years!*] Saw large numbers of prospective confirmation candidates today. Rawlins & I have decided to go to London on DEC 5th. ...

Saturday 5th November

The boys played All Saints', on their own ground, & lost again. It was a perfect autumn afternoon, with lovely cloud effects. We were in fields down the other side of the river – which are inundated in due season. The ball fell into the river after one mighty kick, & they made a lovely picture swarming down the bank & throwing in a lifebelt for it. It was sailing away at a good speed too – Dennis Grivell <u>would</u> have been annoyed! [*Presumably the owner of the ball.*] Fr Bird came along & his kids. It was the little girl who got into the paper by falling into the river & being fished out by a choirboy. When I came away at 4.30 we were leading by 4-3 – & that should have been the end – they'd been playing since just 3 o/c. So it wd have been a win, had they not foolishly gone on, & lost about 5 o/c by 7-6!! Alwyn came & told me the news in the middle of my tea; sunset over the Abbey. Fr Roach walked by.

I took 2 churchings after Evensong – according to the Vicar's peculiar method.

This refers to the service for The Thanksgiving of Women after Childbirth, which may be found in the Book of Common

Prayer – but we have no record of "the Vicar's peculiar method"!

Sunday 6th November – within Octave of All Saints

Children's Mass at 10 – choosing my own hymns (the celebrant's privilege here!) and when I choose 'em, they sing up well! <u>Most</u> of the congregation candidates came at 4 o/c, to arrange classes, etc.

Monday 7th November

Eclipse of the moon tonight. It went red all over, & nearly disappeared. Audrey's photo arrived this morning – hooray!

Friday 11th November

Took my first Confirmation Class tonight – rather good. They were all good (fortunately!). Only a bit of scuffling before we began. Twelve of 'em. 18 more on Sundays. I gave them Fr Ellis's introductory talk – which I consider beyond praise! Mark Brown came – & was impressed.

Sunday 13th November

Sang the Masses at 10 & 11 today. The 11 o/c was very nice – afterwards Geoff & Irene Young want to be confirmed. Evensong at the Abbey – the Bishop preaching – place crammed to the doors – extra seats under the Tower – not enough hymns & prayer books – numbers of the confm. Boys – & I had to go to the

P.H., where there were 6 of us in all. But it was nice all the same – we sang *Now the day is over* & Mr Bourne said he'd sung dozens of babies to sleep with that 'ymn. Then the Bish came to supper (& Young) – all very nice. Poor Dennis Grivell, who doesn't want to be confirmed – I shan't push him. His bro' & sister never made even their 1st Communion. £7.12.0 collection tonight – an average of 2 ½ – or nearly 3d each.

Saturday 19th November

Letter from home, just as I was setting out to the choirboys' football – I now have a baby step-brother! [*FW's father had remarried in the early 1930s, and the half-brother was called Raymond.*] And they want me to go & baptise him. This afternoon on the Column Field, we played S. Chad's – & won, for the first time this season – 6-2. They brought a capable ref with them, & it was a good game – quite a hard one, tho' we won by so much. And tonight I have been favoured by a social visit from Peter Ford & Gordon Backhouse!

Sunday next before Advent, 1938

Said Mass @ 8. Preached + Mattins at Oxon, at 11 – for Fr Renfree, who went to see his son confirmed at school. By bike thro' the rain – good cong, but v. dull service – during the lessons I had bright wavy lines jumping all over the page – & a splitting headache ever since. Got soaked thro' on the way back. SS rather good – an exceptionally small class, as 20 of my boys went "up" to Young. Some new ones next week from the P.H. One Fr Quarrell preached tonight, from ACS,

& I merely read the lessons – but they were good. [*Herbert Quarrell was General Secretary of the Additional Curates Society, and had come up from London.*] Nearly a pew full of confirmation boys, & some at the P.H. too.

Thursday 24th November

In case I ever need to know, Eric Evans is the name of the boy I met at Miss Loxton's "send off" tonight.

Sunday (Advent 1938)

The Oxon cold incubated a bit, & has now come out strong – very strong! Yesterday slept all afternoon. Then at 6 o/c the S.E.C.M., under Dr Nicolson, had a big festival (Evensong). The choirs all sat in the Nave, & the rest of the nave was quite filled with people. [*School of English Church Music. The school was based at Chislehurst, Kent, but it had an association of affiliated churches who committed themselves to the attainment of high standards. After the war it became the Royal School of Church Music.*] A really good do – procession, with copes. A protty man who was deaconed in October was there (Brierley Hill). [*An area of the Black Country south of Dudley, presumably where the Protestant deacon came from!*] 4 or 5 of the boys, including John Lee, came in & we played games – as quietly as possible! Today, sang the children's Mass, & preached at the PH from notes only – about 20 people gave the exceptional collection of 6/7d!

Tuesday 29 November '38 S. Andrew's Eve

For the first time we tried the experiment of a "plan" for continuous intercession, but only got about ½ dozen signatures. Yesterday saw Mrs Hilditch in Berrington Hospital (with Mrs F & Rawlins). She has eczema <u>very</u> badly – it was quite a shock tonight. I suppose leprosy is worse! Tonight's filmshow & lecture about lepers at the Morris Hall. Mrs French very horrified about Trevor Levekin – what he taught her Eric, at school! Mrs F is one of the best. [*Nothing has been found to show who Trevor Levekin was, nor why Mrs French should have been horrified.*]

Wednesday 30th November S. Andrew 1938

The 9.30 Mass – then to Walsall, with things for S. Andrews' Bazaar made by Barbara Elliott, & to baptise the new baby – it had never dawned on me that it wd be their Patronal Festival, but Solemn Evensong wasn't till 8 o/c. All went well, Cyril & Vic & Mabel were godparents [*two of FW's brothers, with the wife of the younger of them*], & Doris & Mrs Somebody also came. Fr Riley did the churching; I bumped my head on the fontcover. I think that's all. Arthur Raymond – he's awfully nice, and quite enjoyed it, especially the actual baptism, [*Added at bottom:* The look of surprise on his face – then he decided he liked it, and laughed!] and when I gave him the end of my stole. [*At that age even a smile must surely have been wind!*]

Lunch at home – then all afternoon at the Vicarage, where they all have colds, & Fr Johnston so bad that he had to stay in – & go to bed early. Bernard I only saw in the vestry last thing. Mrs Leach is making a set of white vestments for a Christmas present for Fr J., & very nice they will be. I only caught the train back at W'ton because it was late – but as it happened I met a boy called Davies who lived in Crowmore Rd – Mrs Tudor is his new stepmother. & what a life he must have lived with that father! However, he's going to the Navy – in about a month's time.

Friday 2nd December

My cold, nearly gone, came back thro' taking a funeral in the pouring rain yesterday! Today John Altrey (not named John) in to tea. PF & AD & BD came in before he left, on their way to Choir practice. He thinks Muriel very nice – says he can pray with her about! Magazines & Confirmation Class – how I enjoy them – I think the boys do too. They ask so many questions we take far longer than we ought. NB. Why not get Tony & those who have holidays, to come & camp in the Vicarage Field at Walsingham?

For the reference to Muriel, see above, September 28th. Tantalising! For Altrey, see above under October 27th.

[*Entry added at top of page:*] SAT: A number of good, but oldish books from the Bray Library at rock bottom prices, by kindness of Dr Lawson.

During the 1690s the Rev Dr Thomas Bray (1656-1730), founder of the SPCK and the SPG, began to establish parochial libraries in every deanery in England and Wales, a project continued after his death by the Associates of Dr Bray. This entry presumably referred to withdrawals from a local clerical lending library.

Advent II 1938

At the back of the church during the early mass (having come by mistake: the Vicar said "What do you want?"!!) I had my eyes opened to one or two things. Mr Adams was the only person who made the slightest attempt to genuflect [*presumably on going up to receive communion*] – that's why he comes up last. Also, the number of people who went out immediately after receiving communion was SEVEN – straight from the altar to the door. However, I don't think it is always as bad as this.

Said the children's Mass, & preached at 11. Tony came (hooray!) so that's one up to me against Mrs W – who reckons he won't keep it up now he's left the choir, but I think he will, & will probably bring Ray Davies. He listened to my sermon – said it was a "sarcy" [*presumably means "sarcastic"*] sermon – so it was! But tonight, oh dear! They were bored stiff for 20 mins by the Vicar – & he [*not clear to whom this refers*] genuinely inquired what it was about. I had to reflect before replying! Congregations both am & pm much better than of late. My "sarcy" sermon was on churchgoing – J.B.D.'s text about Gotham! [*Unknown, unfortunately.*]

Tea with Young at Miss Ormiston's. We <u>were</u> going
to make up a party to see *Busman's Honeymoon* at the
Free Theatre – but the Sale of Work has bunkered it.

Busman's Honeymoon was the play by Dorothy L Sayers and
Muriel St Clare Byrne, later made into a novel by the former,
in which Lord Peter Wimsey and his new wife find their
honeymoon interrupted by the discovery of a corpse in the
cellar. It ran in London from December 1936 for nine months,
and had only just been released for amateur production. FW
enjoyed the works of Dorothy L Sayers – an enthusiasm he
passed on to his elder son – and it is frustrating that we miss
the chance of seeing what he might have said about her play.
The reviewer in the *Shrewsbury Chronicle* liked this production,
which was by the Shrewsbury Dramatic Society and was put
on in the Workingmen's Hall, though he did say that some
of Peter's whimsical comments failed to penetrate to the back
because the audience were laughing at the comic chimney-
sweep. However, the dramatic climax "gripped and thrilled
the audience". In the *Chronicle*'s photograph Wimsey is easily
recognisable – he looks strikingly like a later and more famous
player of the role, Edward Petherbridge!

I got away from the Vicarage early & went round to
the Lovell's to explain (tomorrow being imposs.) and
those photo's <u>may</u> turn up soon, but Joan of course had
never given it another thought. [*It is not known what
this refers to.*] Tony, at the door, at about 10.30. "I
couldn't be miserable if I tried." Me (taken aback) "Oh,
you're a happy child, are you?" Him "Yes" (yawn).

Monday 5th December

By excursion (7.40) to London. 14/6. Rawlins was coming, but is away for a week instead. Funny man in the train, drinking brandy all the time – & his wife eating ham sandwiches. Neither gave the other any. And coming back, I was alone for the whole journey with a man who was certainly not all there. He kept going out for 1/2 an hour at a time, then coming back. He struck about 12 matches for no reason whatever. Ate figs out of a little box. Got a piece of paper & scrubbed nearly half the floor of the compartment with it, & then put it back in his pocket. He pulled down all the blinds, including the one in my corner, without saying a word, and sharpened a knife on some sort of pocket grindstone. He didn't exchange a single word, & he went on past Shrewsbury. At Sh'y 3 sailors got out – & found they had 2 1/2 hours to wait for the next train to Welshpool. Going 7.40-11.0. Coming back 12.10-5.30! [*A very long day!*]

Audrey was waiting at Paddington, & we went first to Kenton, saw the church (magnificent) & had lunch with her mother, the rest of the family being at work. Coming out afterwards we met the Vicar, Fr Johnson, who proved to be exactly what one expected – jolly good. Then to Madame Tussauds, which we enjoyed immensely, wandered all the way from there to Piccadilly, a meal at Lyons (Corner House) which was VERY welcome – then to the Piccadilly Theatre – *George & Margaret* – which was excellent. Altogether the whole day was marvellous. Saw her off at 11.30 from Paddington. Must try it again after Xss – then at Easter

I shall be at the Daniels' at Hornsey – & in the summer
she will come to W'ham quite apart from the scouts.

George and Margaret was a comedy by Gerald Savory, which
had a successful run in the West End at the time but would
seem very dated now.

Saturday 10th December

"We" instituted the new Vicar of S. Alkmund's today
at 3 pm – a terrible experience – howling choir,
wheezing organ, floodlighting from the floor in the
Sanctuary, the appalling east window, the Bp of Stafford
going all lah-de-dah & explaining the service, Holt
looking awfully parsonic, the new Vicar, with red hair
& big glasses, a mere child – he little knows what he's
taken on – & they say he's fearfully protestant – Fr
Mackenzie winking – the congregation about half filling
the church & singing very congregationally – mostly
women & old at that – a cup of perfectly foul tea in
the PAHRISH HAWL – that server from All Saints
who "ain't hardly all there" buttonholing me & Fr M.
Fr M spoke about our choir – said the churchwardens
have power to evict them. Fr (ie Mr) Newby, of S.
Julian's, has been defending the Catholic Faith!!! He's
on an Interdenominational Do, & said he couldn't carry
on unless the Unitarians and Christian Scientists were
eliminated! Result, abusive letters from the Unitarian
minister, & he was asking Fr M & the Rural Dean if
they approved of his action.

An interesting diatribe! St Alkmund's church is dominated
by the chancel window, painted (not stained) by Francis

Eginton of Birmingham in 1795, an allegorical picture showing a figure of faith, rising from the Cross and seeking the crown of glory. The design is copied from the Madonna in Guido Reni's *Assumption of the Blessed Virgin* at Munich. It is more usually regarded as beautiful than appalling! Eginton also worked at St George's Chapel, Windsor, and Salisbury and Lichfield cathedrals. The new vicar was the Revd Sidney Austerberry. For Mr Newby of St Julian's, see above, entry for 19th August.

Sunday Advent III 1938

Only 6 of the Friday Confirmation Class were not at Mass. For the Sunday batch we shall have to wait till next week. Then, <u>when</u> we have got them regular, we can take our choice & have a proper servers' Rota, & dispense with the services of some we now have! Of course the vicar thinks we shan't get them to Mass regularly. I certainly shouldn't like to present any who don't. Maybe I will refuse.

Friday 23rd December

Feels like Saturday – but that's Christmas. Thaw today after several days' terrific frost. Day school parties yesterday & the day before, jolly good. Vicar waiting (in the vestry) for confessions that never came. The Xss [*i.e. Christmas*] Tree arrived at last. Much shopping, & Xss cards, so many extra having sent to me – I've 34 already. Sent to the Confirmation boys (& a few others) – Alwyn, & Edgar Jones delivered 'em for me – after sampling the ginger wine made from Mr Harrison's essence, not half so good as Mrs Holden's.

Apparently there are several from the boys in the post – Alwyn says he nearly put "Mr" – & then remembered "Revd" – not, alas! "Fr". A crowd of us upon the organ at midday while Mr Turner played *Chorus of Shepherds* and a Toccata. Personally I thoroughly enjoy Christmas.

Saw *Snow White & the 7 D's* on Wednesday, but didn't think such a lot of it. Frightfully clever, of course. But I disliked SW & her accent, & loathed the dwarfs & their accents. But the witch scenes were awfully good. Back by the river (as always from the flicks) – full of floating chunks of ice.

One of the most famous of all films, the first full-length cartoon, it was made by Walt Disney in 1937. The accents of the dwarfs are said to be backwoods Kentucky. The voice of Snow White was Adriana Caselotti, who was born in Bridgeport, Connecticut. She earned just $970 for her work on the film, and her only subsequent film role was a brief off-camera speaking part in *The Wizard of Oz*.

Christmas Eve, 1938

Much warmer – but still cold in church – morning flitting about town – Wooly's for toys for the tree. Not as many as last year – well, poor Bruce's 5/- always accounted for ten. Afternoon mostly putting them on the tree & helping the decorators. In the absence of the usual ones Mrs W did the font better than it's ever looked – if only she were not so loud voiced about it! Young says how worried she was to see me showing Albert Harley [*Muriel's brother, FW's future brother-in-law*] how to serve tomorrow. She said "Doesn't he know how to serve after all these years?" And Young said "No". Remark followed about "fuss". Eg, say I, standing for the Gospel, instead of kneeling as he actually did on the only occasion he served a low Mass before!

"Except at the two gospels, and when he is moving about to perform some duty, he [the server at Low Mass] is always kneeling." *Ritual Notes*, 8th edition. FW means that Albert should have stood but in fact knelt for the Gospel.

While at S. Mary's for my confession – all the lights in the town went out, so I had to make it in the dark. Woolworth's was lit by gas – so I got the electric fittings for the Crib. Just because Tom Brown hadn't turned up with his flex, etc, nobody was going to do it. So Mr Adams & I spent an hour and a half – we did something wrong – because it won't go off! Evidently we have had a narrow escape, somehow! We've compromised by taking one of the bulbs out. They are very low power (5 watts) & consequently not very bright, but there couldn't have been much light in the Stable, & anyway it means we can leave them on permanently.

Christmas cards from Ray Davis, & Alwyn Dickson – "with love from Alwyn & Margaret". God bless them. Keep them O Lord as the apple of an eye – hide them under the shadow of Thy wings. [*Psalm 17, v. 8.*]

CHRISTMAS DAY, 1938

Up at 6 o/c – got my own water & shaved etc downstairs. In church 6.30. Said Mass 7, assisted at 8. 82 at 7 – & only 69 at 8. Ray H & Colin came, but not Mostyn. At 11 (High Mass) everything went beautifully – nearly all my confirmation boys were there, & a good number of SS children. I've never had such a happy Sunday morning at the Abbey. Tony & Ray D & David Lee came in for some ginger wine – Xss cards from them. Peter Ford brought me a 1/- pkt of Players from himself & Gordon Backhouse – & Doug Thomas, who is so very poor, insisted on my having a large orange as a Xss present. David Lee wouldn't have any ginger wine – shortbread instead – & Tony was sure it wasn't as good as Mrs Holden's! He was greatly grieved that I hadn't any decorations – but was impressed at the number of cards! 72. They are coming to the Xss Social, but we can't go to the Panto together, as he & Ray are already going to both B'ham & W'ton [*Birmingham and Wolverhampton*]!

Well, last night I couldn't sleep, and so when Mark & his girl knocked at 11.20 – I accompanied them to Midnight Mass at S. Mary's – shan't go again. So irreverent – unavoidable in the C of E, I suppose! Their ticket scheme didn't work, & a sidesman actually asked me, was I going up to receive? So I said "NO!" It was a High Mass, but not very impressive, & the choir were awful. Blessing the Crib done properly. You expect to see a few drunks on Xss Eve, but we met a poor laddie of about 16 – a mere kid, on Wyle Cop – & I couldn't get him out of my mind all thro' Mass. If Tony or one of my boys did that on Xss Eve! Sacred Heart of Jesus, have mercy on us. God bless them all.

Cards from Brian & Tommy, presented shyly before Mass. Young rushed off in great haste to catch the 12.45

train home (afraid to go by road). [*A train on Christmas Day! Needless to say, it couldn't be done today!*] To Prestfelde for tea & supper, where was Mr Turner (& his daughter) whom I met at the Missionary exhibition. It turns out he was Mr Dovey's headmaster at Wimbledon. A jolly good supper (duck). In bed by 12.20. Far more people at Evensong cum Carols than I would have expected. Coming down the Foregate from Prestfelde I overheard a girl saying to her parents "I'm glad it comes on a Sunday – you can forget it more easily – after all, Christmas doesn't mean much to us". Such a contrast to my own happy day.

BOXING DAY

Said Mass of S. Stephen at 11 – served by Ray Lewis. Alwyn came in to arrange about the Pantomime. A jolly good time with the Thomas's at Meole. Then the Vicarage Xss dinner – very good. Mrs W's sister not over this time. Dennis Pugh over from Shirlett [*near Bridgenorth*] for Xss. The Abbot of Buckfast has died.

A Community of English Benedictines, refounded in 1882 on the site of a mediaeval monastery in Devon. The abbot in question was Anscar Vonier, who had been abbot since 1906, and whose life's work was the building of the abbey church, using only the labour of the monks themselves. The church had been consecrated in 1932.

Thus ends the diary. Frank Wain went on to serve his second curacy at St Andrew's, Walsall, and in early 1942 went out to the West Indies, taking a long and indirect route to avoid the German U-boats. He served at Biabou, St Vincent, where he was responsible for building a church (by the sea, in possibly the most beautiful setting in the world!), which is well cherished by the local people over half a century later, and then in Grenada. After returning to England, in 1950 he married Muriel Harley, by then a primary school teacher in Surrey. After brief spells in the Lichfield diocese and in Coventry, he went to the parishes of Kinwarton, Great Alne and Haselor, in rural Warwickshire, where he remained till his retirement in 1983. Amongst his interests was ecclesiastical (as well as general) history. Muriel died in 1999 and Frank in 2002.

In auctoris memoria et ad gloriam Auctoris

Some of the clergy, with their livings in 1938

Alexander Agnew, Vicar of St George's, Shrewsbury.

Albert Bird, Vicar of All Saints', Shrewsbury.

Cyril Butler, Rector of Frodesley, Shrewsbury.

Wilfrid Ellis, Vicar of St George's, Wolverhampton. Between 1925 and 1935 he had served in what was then Northern Rhodesia, being at one time provost of the Cathedral Church of Ndola.

Edgar Foizey, Vicar of St Michael & All Angels, Caldmore, Walsall.

Luke Freeman, a tutor at the Theological College, Lichfield.

John Goodacre, Vicar of Mountford, Shrewsbury.

Victor Hambling, Vicar of Fillongley, Coventry, 1936-38, and of St Matthew's, Leicester from 1938.

Thomas Hannay, Principal of the College of the Resurrection since 1933. His earlier ministry had included a period working in Africa from 1914 to 1927. In 1942 he became Bishop of Argyll and the Isles.

William Hassall, Vicar of St Stephen's, Wolverhampton.

Morley Headlam, Vicar of Atcham and Rural Dean of Shrewsbury.

Donald Holt, Curate of St Alkmund's, Shrewsbury, ordained at the same time as FW.

Thomas Hulme, Vicar of St George's, Walsall.

Kenneth Millington, Vicar of St Mary's & All Saints, Palfrey, Walsall, from 1938.

Leonard Newby, Vicar of St Julian's, Shrewsbury, from 1916.

Charles Norcock, Rector of Wentnor, Shropshire. In 1938
he became Vicar of Breinton, Herefordshire.

Charles Ravizotti, Vicar of St Mark's, Walsall.

Jack Rawlins, Curate of St Chad's, Shrewsbury from 1938,
ordained the same year as FW.

Russell Renfree, Vicar of Shelton with Oxon.

Harry Richardson, College of the Resurrection 1932, ordained
priest 1935, Curate of Outwood, Wakefield to 1938, of
Leeds from 1938.

Henry Riley, curate at St Andrew's, Walsall, since 1937.
Previously curate of St Luke's, Pallion, Sunderland.

Charles Roach, Vicar of St Chad's, Shrewsbury from 1938.

Geoffrey Soden, Rector of St James', Wednesbury.

Adrian Stokes, Rector of Acton Burnell with Pitchford.

Arthur Talbot, Vicar of Rushall since as early as 1909.

Percy Turner, Rector of Wem.

Loughton Wilkinson, Vicar of Holy Cross, Shrewsbury (The
Abbey).

Stan Young, Curate of Holy Cross, Shrewsbury (The Abbey).
In 1942 he became Chaplain and in 1949 Headmaster.
of Prestfelde School, Shrewsbury

Select Bibliography

Crockford's Clerical Directory.

F L Cross and E A Livingstone, *The Oxford Dictionary of the Christian Church*, 2nd ed. Oxford UP, 1974.

Roy Jenkins, *Churchill*, Macmillan, 2001.

R J C Lumley, *The Abbey of Saint Peter and Paul and Parish Church of the Holy Cross, Shrewsbury; historical and descriptive handbook*, The British Publishing Co.

The *Mirfield Gazette.*

Stanley Morison, *The History of The Times*, Vol. 4, pt.2, The 150th anniversary and beyond, 1921-1948, *The Times*, 1952.

An oral history of St Andrew's Church, Birchills, Walsall, 1887-1987.

Pictures of the English Liturgy, Catholic Literature Association, 1922.

Howell Rees, *Tour of Shrewsbury Sights*, 2000.

Andrew Roberts, *Emininent Churchillians*, Weidenfeld and Nicolson, 1994.

The *Shrewsbury Chronicle.*

Colin Stephenson, *Walsingham Way*, Darton, Longman & Todd, 1970.

A J P Taylor, *English History, 1914-1945*, Oxford UP, 1965.

Alan Wilkinson, *The Community of the Resurrection; a centenary history*, SCM Press, 1992.